hand-crafted cards

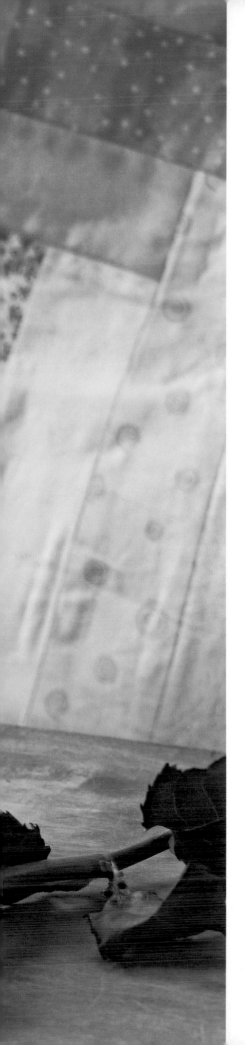

hand-crafted cards

50 step-by-step projects for every celebration

Emma Hardy

CICO BOOKS

LONDON NEW YORK

For my two gorgeous girls, Gracie and Betty

This edition published in 2014 by CICO Books
An imprint of Ryland Peters & Small Ltd
519 Broadway, 5th floor, New York, NY 10012
20-21 Jockey's Fields, London WC1R 4BW

First published in 2005 by CICO Books under the title *Fast, Fun Cards*

www.rylandpeters.com

10 9 8 7 6 5 4 3 2 1

Text copyright © Emma Hardy 2005
Design and photography © CICO Books 2005

A CIP catalog record for this book is available from the Library of
Congress and the British Library.

ISBN: 978 1 78249 091 3

Editor: Gillian Haslam
Designer: David Fordham
Photographer: Tino Tedaldi (pages 88, 90, 110, and 114 by Jacqui Hurst)
Stylist: Georgina Harris

Printed in China

Contents

Introduction   6

General Greetings Cards   10

Children's Cards   76

Special Occasions   92

Introduction

The tradition of sending greetings cards stretches back over 200 years, although hand-written valentine cards were sent much earlier. Originally favored by the wealthy, these early cards were extremely intricate and elaborate designs, and were consequently quite expensive. They were usually hand delivered, but as postal services grew, the trend of sending greetings cards became more widespread. Printers and manufacturers improved their printing methods and by the 1850s more affordable cards had become widely available.

Today, greetings cards are hugely popular, and are sent for a wide range of occasions. There is nothing more special than a handmade card, which shows thought and effort in a way that a store-bought card cannot do. In this book, you will find 50 different card designs with many variations that can be made with your own personal touches to suit any occasion, from a child's birthday to a valentine card for a loved one, from a thank-you notelet to Christmas cards that can be made in bulk.

Making cards

Most of the cards are very simple to create and many are suitable for children to make themselves. Some specific craft techniques are used, such as quilling, fringing, and teabag folding, but these are shown in clear step-by-step photographs and are easily mastered. Only basic craft materials are used, and if you gather

a collection of scraps of pretty papers, fabric, ribbon, and braid, you'll always be able to create a unique card within minutes.

When creating a one-off card for a specific occasion, time can be spent on it to make it truly special, but when several cards are required, such as Christmas and thank-you cards, the designs need to be kept simple so that they are quick and easy to make. As an alternative to making multiples of a greetings card, make one card and scan it into a computer. Print out several copies, or try photocopying the image for similar results.

Choosing paper and other materials

Most of the materials used in this book are readily available from craft stores. Start to collect pretty gift wrapping papers and craft papers in a range of colors to use in future designs. Cards generally use only small amounts of paper, fabric, ribbons, and braids, so keep scraps left over from other craft projects.

When choosing card, ensure that it is the required weight for the purpose. If it is to be used for the backing card, make sure that it is thick enough to stand up, and use thinner card and paper if sticking several layers together to avoid a bulky finish.

Standard water-based craft glue is used throughout the projects in this book. Glue stick is used for sticking flat pieces of thin card together, while high-tack, fast-drying glue is used to stick thick card together and to fix ribbons and buttons in place. Spray adhesive is useful for sticking thin tissue paper onto card and

TOP: Glittery Bird Card
(page 134)
ABOVE: Ribbon Notelet
(page 144)

will give a neat, flat finish. However, it does have a strong smell and has to be used in a very well-ventilated space.

Equipment and basic techniques

It is worth investing in a good cutting mat, a sharp craft knife, and metal ruler for the best results when cutting card. A pair of sharp scissors is required when cutting out shapes from paper and card, and use small scissors such as embroidery scissors for more intricate cuts. Scissors with shaped blades are now widely available and come in a range of designs to create interesting edgings and borders. It is best to keep one pair of scissors for cutting paper and card, and another pair for cutting fabric and ribbon, to avoid blunting the blades.

The most effective way of folding a card with a neat crease is to score along the fold line. To do this, gently run the craft knife along the ruler on the line, using only gentle pressure. Do not cut through the card. Always score along what will be the inside of the card for a neat fold on the outside.

When using the templates at the back of this book, simply trace off the shape if it is the required size, or photocopy the templates, enlarging as required.

Take inspiration from the designs and projects in this book, either copying the cards or creating your own variations, and enjoy creating some very special greetings cards to give to family and friends, who will surely treasure them for many years to come.

ABOVE LEFT: Patchwork Card (page 64)
ABOVE RIGHT: Vintage Wallpaper Card (page 22)

General Greetings Cards

This chapter is packed with more than twenty projects, providing ideas for greetings cards suitable for all occasions, from birthdays to party invitations, from thank-you notes to get-well greetings. The projects illustrate how you can turn even the smallest scrap of pretty fabric, ribbon, or wallpaper into a striking card, and how you can use equipment such as scissors with shaped blades or hole punches to create special finishing touches. The techniques featured include embossing, spray painting, applying metal leaf, and simple ribbon embroidery and patchwork.

Vintage Flower Button Card

Collect old buttons in pretty colors and shapes
to make this lovely flower card with a vintage feel. Rickrack is used to continue the
haberdashery theme, with the decoration carried over to the back of the card to add an extra-
special touch. Use buttons and braid of a similar color or glue on a group of flower-shaped
buttons in different colors to create a miniature garden on a card.

Materials

Piece of thin card

A selection of flower-
    shaped buttons
    (seven flowers and
    one leaf)

Rickrack braid in three
    different colors

16-in (40.5-cm) length
    of ⅛-in (3-mm) wide
    satin ribbon

Fabric glue

Craft knife, cutting mat,
    and metal ruler

Pencil

Needle and thread

Scissors

Tip

Try arranging the
flowers into a bouquet
for a different look.

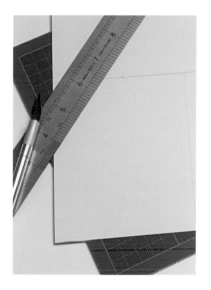

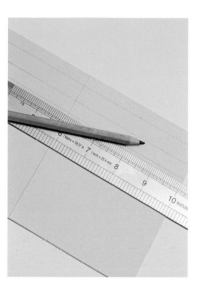

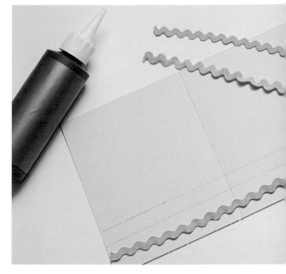

1 Cut out a rectangle of card measuring 8¼ x 5¼in (21 x 13.5cm). Score a line across the middle of the card.

2 Draw a faint line ½in (1cm) up from and parallel to the bottom edge, a second line ⅝in (15mm) above from the first line, and a third line ½in (1cm) up from the second line.

3 Cut the rickrack into three lengths to fit across the card (both front and back) and glue each piece to cover a pencil line. Leave to dry.

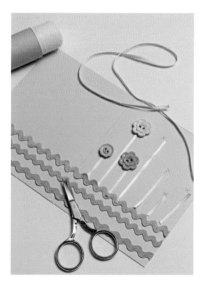

4 Arrange the buttons on the card front and mark the position of each one with a pencil. Cut a length of ribbon to make each flower stem and glue in place, tucking the bottom edge under the top line of rickrack. Leave to dry.

5 Stitch each button in place on top of a stem, taking the thread through each button twice from the back and tying the ends with a knot on the inside.

6 Cut out a piece of card measuring 4¼ x 5¼in (10.5 x 13.5cm) and glue to the inside of the card front to hide the thread. Fold the greetings card along the scored fold line.

Teacup Card

Invite friends to tea with these cute cup-and-saucer cards.
Using papers with a small pattern, the simple shapes are cut and glued onto a backing card to give a distinctly homespun, patchwork feel. Vary the number of cups to make a range of greetings cards in different sizes, some featuring just one cup and saucer, and others with two or three placed horizontally or vertically.

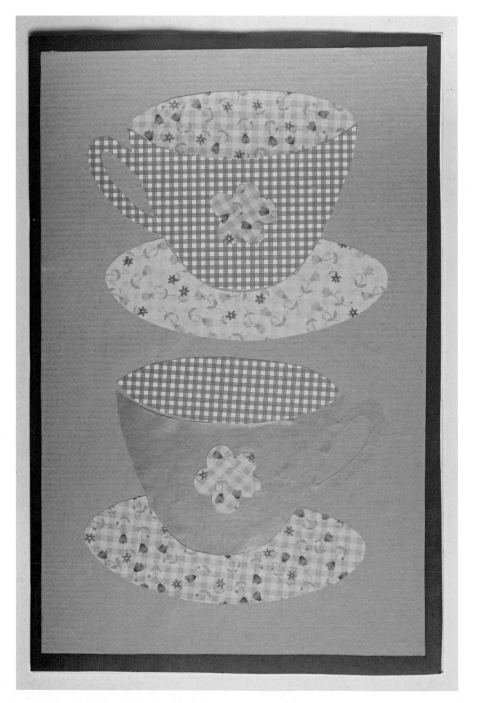

Materials

Thin cream card
Paper in pale blue and
    bright pink
Selection of patterned
    papers
Scrap paper
Craft knife, cutting mat,
    and metal ruler
Pencil
Scissors
Glue stick

Tip

If you have scraps of fabric that you would like to use for these greetings cards, simply iron fusible webbing to the back of them. Cut out the cups and saucers using the templates, and glue onto the backing card as in step 3.

1 Photocopy the templates on page 147 and cut out. Draw around the templates onto patterned papers, partnering different papers together to make a pleasing arrangement, and cut out. You will need one cup in each design, one matching saucer for both cups, and two insides of cups for each card. Flower motifs can be cut to decorate the cards if you wish.

2 Cut out a rectangle of blue paper measuring 5¼ × 8¼in (13.5 × 21cm), using the craft knife and metal ruler.

3 Position the cups, saucers, and other pieces onto the blue paper rectangle and glue in place with glue stick. Press down firmly to give a smooth finish.

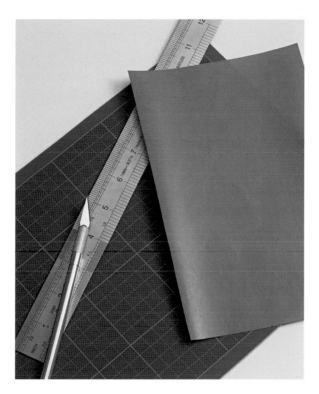

4 Cut out a rectangle of bright pink paper measuring 5½ x 8½ in (14 x 22cm), using the craft knife and metal ruler.

5 Cut out a rectangle of cream card measuring 11 x 8½ in (28 x 22cm). Score down the center, 5½ in (14cm) from each side and fold in half.

6 Stick the front of the card to the cream folded card using glue stick, smoothing it down carefully for a neat, flat finish.

Metallic Circles Card

Make this card with simple circles of metallic wrapping paper used to great effect. Cut the circles from any kind of paper—you could try using patterned or striped papers for a different effect—or use up scraps of fabric.

Materials

Thin card in plum and
cream
Metallic gift-wraps in
four colors
Scrap paper
Glue stick
Craft knife, cutting mat,
and metal ruler
Compass and pencil
8¼-in (21-cm) length of
¼-in (7-mm) wide
green ribbon
Scissors

Tip

Try making an envelope
from one of the
wrapping papers for a
stylish finishing touch.

1 Using the compass, draw a
circle ¾in (2cm) in diameter on
scrap paper and cut out. Using the
circle as a template, draw around
it onto the metallic papers, cutting
four circles of each color.

2 Cut out a square of cream
card measuring 5 × 5in (13 ×
13cm). Arrange the circles
onto the card, leaving about
⅛in (3mm) between each and
ensuring that no two circles of
the same color are next to each
other. Glue the circles in place
with glue stick.

3 Cut out a rectangle of colored
card measuring 5¼ × 10½in
(13.5 × 27cm). Score a line down
the center of the card, 5¼in
(13.5cm) from each side, and fold
in half. Glue the decorated panel
to the front of this, ensuring an
even border all the way around.

4 Tie the length of ribbon into a
neat, flat bow. Trim the ends with
scissors to prevent them fraying
and glue in place on the card.

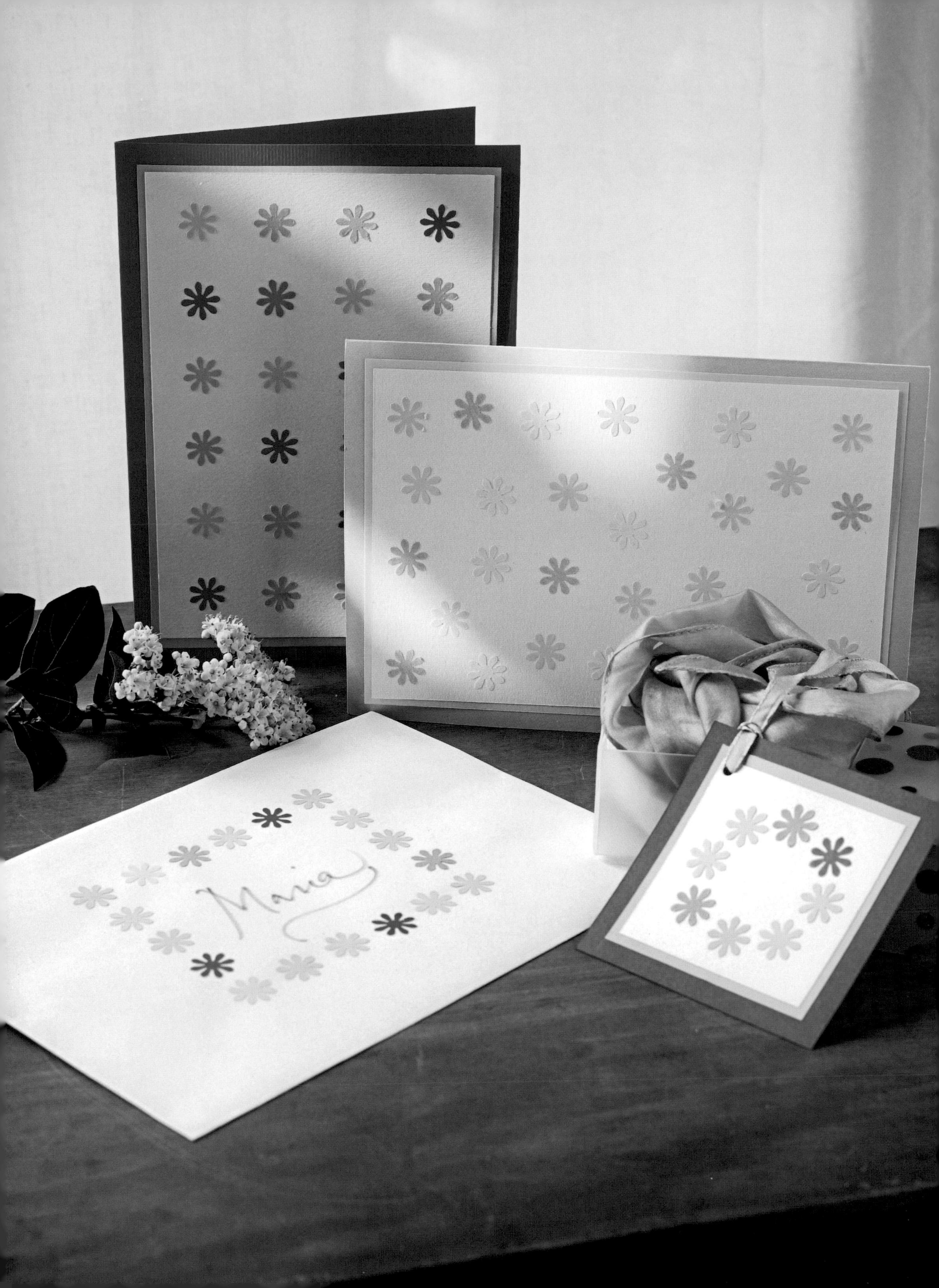
Maria

Flower Stamp Card

Use the paper shapes produced by a decorative hole punch to create these attractive flower cards. Choose shades of pink and lilac or green and pale blue for a fresh, modern look. Either place the flowers in regular lines or create a more random design, but always ensure that colors are separated.

Materials

Thin card in bright pink, lilac,
   and cream
Co-ordinating colored papers
   (about five different colors)
Flower paper stamp
Glue stick
Craft knife, cutting mat, and
   metal ruler
Pencil

Tip

Make smaller versions to use as gift tags, or decorate envelopes to match.

1 Cut out a rectangle of cream card measuring 4⅞ × 7¼ in (12.5 × 18.5cm).

2 Punch out flowers from colored papers using the paper stamp. You will need 24 flowers in total, in different colors.

3 Arrange the flowers onto the cream card, making six lines of four flowers, ensuring that no flowers of the same color are placed next to each other. Stick them in place, using glue stick.

4 Cut out a rectangle of lilac card measuring 5¼ × 7⅝ in (13.5 × 19.4cm) and glue it behind the cream card.

5 Cut out a rectangle of pink card measuring 12 × 8½ in (30.5 × 22cm). Score down the center of the card, 6in (15.25cm) from each side, and fold in half. Stick the front of the card to this.

Vintage Wallpaper Card

$\mathcal{T}$ake yourself back in time to your grandmother's parlor
with this vintage-style card utilizing a motif from a classic wallpaper panel. The simplicity
of this greetings card is enhanced by the old-fashioned charm of the design.

Materials

Piece of thin card

Scrap of old wallpaper

Length of ribbon

Spray adhesive

Craft knife, cutting mat, and
    metal ruler

Hole punch

Scissors

1 Cut out a rectangle of wallpaper 5¼ x 3¾in (13.5 x 9.5cm) and a rectangle of card measuring 11½ x 3½in (29 x 9cm).

Tip

Use new wallpaper with a vintage feel, or collect scraps of original wallpapers. Modern gift-wraps in traditional designs will work well too.

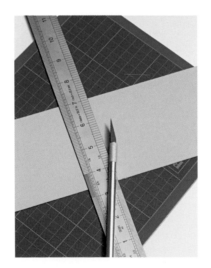

2 Working in a well-ventilated area, spray adhesive to the back of the wallpaper and stick it to the right-hand end of the card so the outside edges match.

3 Score a line across the middle of the card and fold the card in half along the line.

4 Punch holes at the top and bottom of the strip along the fold on the card front. Thread ribbon through the holes and tie in a bow on the front, trimming the ends.

Embossed Card

Stylish and simple, this card is made using

a store-bought embossing sheet and embossing tool. The finished result is very effective, and although very easy to do, takes some patience to produce a perfect result. Choose a long, narrow pattern, which can be repeated if it is not long enough, and emboss onto medium-weight paper. The paper will easily tear if too thin, and will not show the embossing if too thick, so experiment with a few different weights of paper to find the right one.

Materials

Thin card in brown,
   cream, and pink
Metal embossing plate
Embossing tool
Tape
Pencil
Craft knife, cutting mat,
   and metal ruler
Scallop-bladed scissors
Glue stick
Rotary hole punch
10-in (25.5-cm) length
   of ½-in (1-cm)
   wide ribbon

1 Cut out a rectangle of pink card measuring 2¾ × 8in (6.5 × 20.5cm). Lay the metal embossing plate on a light box or tape it to a window with plenty of light shining through. Position the pink card over the embossing plate, ensuring that the design is centered.

2 Using the embossing tool, draw around the pattern on the embossing plate. Work slowly but firmly, making sure all the detail is picked out. Continue to work around the entire pattern.

3 If a larger pattern is required, remove the card when the whole design has been embossed and reposition the card where required, taping it in place so that it will not move while being worked on. Emboss the rest of the card. Remove the tape.

4 Cut out a rectangle of cream card measuring 3½ × 8in (9 × 20.5cm). Lightly draw a pencil line ¼in (7mm) in from each long side and cut along this with the scalloped scissors to make a pretty edging.

5 Cut out a rectangle of brown card measuring 8 × 9in (20.5 × 23cm). Score a line down the center of the card 4½ in (11.5cm) in from each long side and fold in half. Using the glue stick, glue the cream card down the center of the front of the brown card, then glue the embossed panel centrally onto this.

6 Punch two small holes at the top of the embossed panel ½ in (1cm) from the top and ½ in (1cm) apart with the hole punch. Thread the ribbon through and tie into a bow. Trim the ends of the ribbon with scissors to neaten them.

Tip
Use the same embossing technique to decorate the flap of the envelope, either home-made or shop-bought, and add a matching ribbon bow for an extra-special detail.

Present Card

Send good wishes with a special gift-wrapped card.
Choose a beautifully patterned paper to use as the background and embellish with an extravagant but easy-to-make bow. Ribbon edged with thin wire is ideal for this card as it holds its shape well and can be bent into the required shape very easily.

Materials
Patterned paper
Thin card in a
   co-ordinating color
Craft knife, cutting mat,
   and metal ruler
1-in (2.5-cm) wide
   wired ribbon:
   20in (51cm) for the
   present and 31½in
   (80cm) for the bow
Fast-drying, high-tack
   craft glue
Glue stick
Needle and thread
Scissors
Pencil

Tip
These cards can be
made to any size.
Make them in different
dimensions, and try
small gift tags, using
thinner ribbon to
make the bow.

1 Measure and cut out an 8½-in (22-cm) square of patterned paper.

2 Cut two 10-in (25.5-cm) lengths of ribbon. Glue ⅝in (15mm) of one length to the back of the patterned paper, glue stick the ribbon across the front of the card, then fold and glue another ⅝in (15mm) to the back of the paper at the other side. Repeat with the second ribbon, gluing it horizontally across the paper.

3 Cut out a rectangle of colored card measuring 8½ × 17in (22 × 43cm). Score down the center of the card, to make the front and back of the card, and fold neatly in half. Using glue stick, glue the card front to this.

4 Using the 31½-in (80-cm) length of ribbon, make a loop about 2½in (6cm) long, then continue to make five more loops of a similar size. Make a few stitches with the needle and thread to hold all the loops in place. Loop the remaining ribbon over itself at the center of the bow, and secure with a few small stitches. Glue onto the center of the card where the ribbons cross.

Coat Hanger Card

T he perfect card for girls—scraps of fabric are used to good effect to make pretty cards with a retro feel. The dress is made from just two pieces of fabric, with only a few stitches needed to create the finished outfit. Choose fabrics with small-scale patterns and a slightly old-fashioned feel to complement the style of the dress. The coat hanger is made with a few twists of silver wire and a small ribbon bow is added for subtle decoration.

Materials

Scraps of pretty fabric
Thin silver jewelry wire
Pliers
⅛-in (3-mm) wide
    ribbon
Thin card in cream
    and pink
Glue stick
Needle and thread
Fast-drying, high-tack
    craft glue
Craft knife, cutting mat,
    and metal ruler

Tip

When making the coat hanger, fold the wire in half and hold the fold with pliers to make twisting the wire easier.

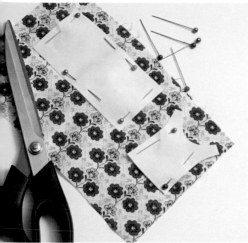

1 Photocopy the top of the dress template and the coat hanger shape from page 147 and cut out. Cut a rectangle for the skirt. Draw around the templates onto fabric and cut out with scissors.

2 Using a needle and thread, make a running stitch along the top of the skirt and gather it up, finishing with a few small stitches so that it measures 1½in (4cm). Stick this to the top using craft glue.

3 Take a 10-in (25.5-cm) length of silver wire. Fold it in half and hold this end with the pliers. Twist the two ends of wire around themselves until you reach the end of the wire.

4 Using the coat hanger template shape, carefully bend the wire to form a coat hanger, pushing the ends through the loop and bending into a hook shape at the top. Trim the ends of the wire neatly.

5 Put a dab of craft glue on each shoulder of the dress and fold them over the coat hanger. Press firmly to stick in position. Cut a rectangle of pink card measuring 6¼ × 10in (16 × 25.5cm). Score down the center of the card 5in (12.75cm) in from each long side and fold in half.

6 Cut a rectangle of cream card measuring 4⅜ × 5½in (11 × 14cm) and glue stick onto the pink card. Apply small dabs of craft glue to the back of the dress and glue onto the card. Finish the card with a small bow, using about 6in (15cm) of ribbon. Attach it to the dress with craft glue.

Windmill Card

Make these simple but very effective paper windmills using patterned papers to create stylish greetings cards. Collect co-ordinating patterned papers—origami papers are ideal as only small pieces are needed for the windmills—and use a plain paper background. Make matching gift tags with just one windmill on each card.

1 Cut out three pieces of patterned paper measuring 2½ x 3½ in (6 x 9cm).

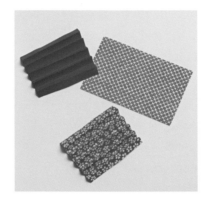

2 Begin folding the paper from one end into a concertina shape, making each fold about ¼ in (7mm) wide.

3 Staple the paper together horizontally across the middle. Cut the ends into a rounded shape using scissors.

4 Open out the windmill and glue the edges together to form a complete circle. Hold the glued edges tightly in place until dry. Make a further two windmills in this way.

5 Cut a 7½ x 5-in (19 x 13-cm) rectangle of paper and a 5½ x 16-in (14 x 40.5-cm) rectangle of cream card. Score down the center of the card, halfway between each short edge and fold in half.

6 Glue the plain paper rectangle onto the front of the cream card using craft glue, then glue the windmills on in your chosen arrangement using a small dab of craft glue.

WINDMILL CARD

Materials

Thin cream card

Three co-ordinating patterned
   papers in similar colors

Plain colored paper for
   background

Stapler and staples

Scissors

Craft knife, cutting mat, and
   metal ruler

Glue stick

Fast-drying, high-tack craft glue

Pencil

Tip

Personal delivery is preferable
for these three-dimensional
cards to prevent the windmills
getting crushed in the mail.

Vintage Fabric Card

This beautifully classic floral fabric

is enhanced within a two-tier contrasting design. A velvet ribbon augments and finishes
the card wonderfully, and the simplicity of the design makes it perfect for any occasion.
Stitching will ensure there is no fraying. This card is a great way to use up and display
favorite vintage fabrics, and to share them with loved ones and friends.

Materials

Thin cream card

Scraps of vintage fabric

14-in (36-cm) length of
⅜-in (9-mm) wide
velvet ribbon

Spray adhesive

Fast-drying, high-tack
craft glue

Craft knife, cutting mat,
and metal ruler

Needle and thread

Scissors

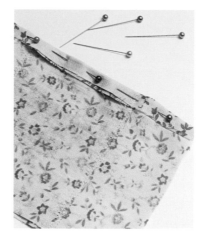

1 Cut out a 4¾ x 3¼ in (12 x 8-cm) piece of fabric and place across the center of a larger piece of fabric measuring 4¾ x 7in (12 x 18cm); pin in place. Work a row of small running stitches along both edges of the smaller piece by hand or work rows of machine zigzag stitches to join them.

2 Press under ¼in (7mm) to the wrong side on all four sides of the assembled fabric and stitch in place with hand running stitches or with a machine straight stitch.

3 Cut out a piece of card measuring 8½ x 6½in (22 x 17cm). Score the card to make the center fold line and fold the card in half. Working in a well-ventilated area, spray adhesive onto the back of the fabric and press it into place onto the front of the card, then leave to dry.

4 Cut two lengths of ribbon to fit across the card and glue them in place to cover the joins, then leave to dry.

5 Make a flat bow from the remaining ribbon by folding a 4¾in (12cm) length into a loop with the ends overlapping by ½in (1cm) at the center back. Stitch through the middle, then wrap another loop of ribbon around the center. Secure with a few stitches to make a bow.

6 Glue the bow to the center of the top line of ribbon and leave to dry.

Fringed Flower Card

These beautiful flower cards are made using a technique called fringing. Little cuts are made along strips of quilling paper, using small bladed scissors, and the strips are then glued around tight coils of paper. Quilling paper is available from many craft suppliers but for the widest choice of colors, contact specialist paper craft companies. Quilling paper is also available with colors graduating from dark to light on each strip, which creates a delicate look for these pretty flowers.

Materials

¼-in (7-mm) wide quilling paper in pale yellow

½-in (1-cm) wide quilling paper in pale lavender (strips of graduating color used here)

⅛-in (3-mm) wide quilling paper in pale green

Thin card in blue and cream

Small scissors

Fast-drying, high-tack craft glue and a small pot

Toothpick

Glue stick

Craft knife, cutting mat, and metal ruler

1 Cut an 18-in (45.5-cm) length of yellow quilling paper in yellow. (If necessary, glue two strips together by slightly overlapping the ends and fixing with a dab of glue.) Coil the strip into a tight coil, rolling it between your fingers, to make the center of the flower, securing the end in place with a dab of craft glue. Make another two flower centers.

2 Measure and cut three 4-in (10-cm) lengths of lavender quilling paper and make small snips with the scissors all the way along. Don't worry too much about getting them even.

3 Glue the end of a 4in (10cm) lavender strip to the center of a flower and hold in place until stuck. Wind the strip around the flower center tightly and stick the end in place by applying a spot of glue with a toothpick. Carefully open out the fringed paper to form petals.

Tip
Try making random patterns using several fringed flowers, rather than placing them on stalks. A simple daisy chain border would work well, or glue them in a circle for a simple wreath shape.

4 Cut out a rectangle of colored card measuring 4 × 4½in (10 × 11.5cm). Cut a strip of green quilling paper, fold in half and curl the ends, sticking it onto the background card to form two stalks. Apply small amounts of craft glue with a cocktail stick. Cut another 3¼-in (8-cm) strip, curl the end, and glue onto the card to make the center stalk.

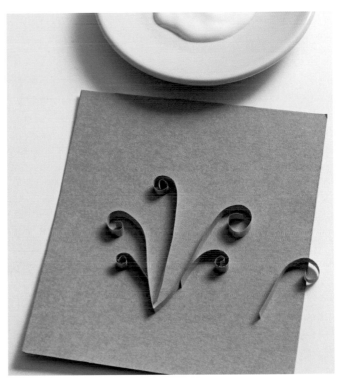

5 Cut three small strips of green quilling paper measuring 1¼–1½in (3–4cm). Curl the ends and glue one onto each stalk.

6 Cut out a rectangle of cream card measuring 4⅜ × 9½in (11 × 24cm), score down the center 4¾in (12cm) from each side, and fold. Glue the front of the card onto this, with the fold of the card at the top. Glue the flowers in place with craft glue.

Paper Collage Leaf Card

The muted colors of this paper-collage card give it a sophisticated feel. Any number of panels can be used in varying sizes to create a collection of greetings cards and gift tags. Brown parcel paper is used and is available in colored versions. Use dark colors for a classic look or try brighter shades for a more colorful version.

Materials

Thin, buff colored card

Craft papers in purple, dark green, brown, and light green

Craft knife, cutting mat, and metal ruler

Scissors

Pencil

Glue stick

1 Photocopy the leaf shapes from page 147 and cut out. Draw around the templates and cut out two light green leaves and one brown oak leaf, cutting out the central cuts with scissors.

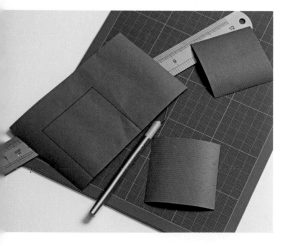

2 Cut out two squares of purple paper measuring 2¾ x 2¾ in (7 x 7cm) and one dark green square of the same size.

3 Glue the leaves onto the paper squares using glue stick, sticking the green leaves on the purple paper and the brown leaf onto the dark green square.

4 Cut out a rectangle of buff-colored card measuring 9 x 6¼ in (23 x 16cm). Score and fold in half lengthways, 3⅛ in (8cm) from each side. Glue the decorated squares in place with glue stick.

Frame Card

This monochrome design enhances black and white photographs.
The template can be photocopied straight from the book for an easy make, or can be photocopied onto colored papers or enlarged or decreased to fit your wishes.

Materials

Thin white card, suitable for
   use in a photocopier
Craft knife, cutting mat, and
   metal ruler
Glue stick
Pencil

Tip

Use the design to frame a
Christmas family photo or any
other special occasion.

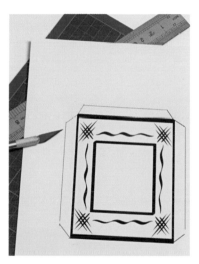

1 Photocopy the template on page 148 onto white card and cut it out using a craft knife and metal ruler. (Check the size of the photocopied frame and adjust the size of the finished card to fit if necessary.)

2 Score the fold lines along each of the three flaps and fold the flaps under to the wrong side.

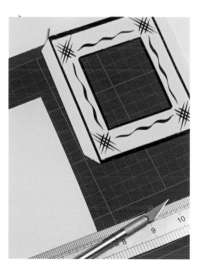

3 Cut out a rectangle of card measuring 10 x 3¾ in (25.5 x 9.5cm) with a craft knife and metal ruler. Score the fold line at the halfway point across the rectangle and fold the card in half.

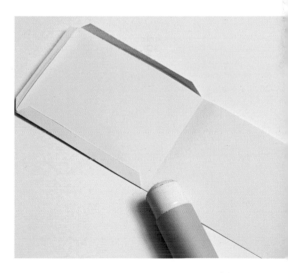

4 Apply glue only to the flaps of the frame, then press into position onto the front of the card and leave to dry. Slide your chosen photograph in through the open edge.

Shirt and Tie Card

Give a shirt and tie with a difference.

Make them in specific colors for male family members and friends, choosing small print gift-wrap for the tie and handkerchief. Use a tracing wheel, usually used to trace sewing pattern pieces, to make a stitching pattern on the front of the shirt, around the collar, and around the pocket. The neat handkerchief provides the finishing touch.

Materials

Thin card in cream
    and red
Cream paper
Patterned gift-wrap
Tracing wheel
Craft knife, cutting mat,
    and metal ruler
Pencil
Fast-drying, high-tack
    craft glue

Tip

For a formal greeting, make a bow tie and waistcoat from paper and glue onto the shirt in place of the tie and pocket.

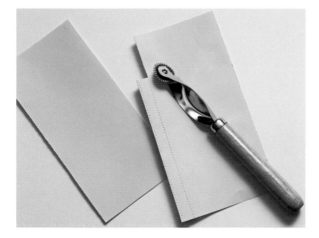

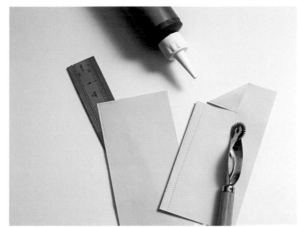

1 Cut out two rectangles of cream paper, one measuring 6 × 2¾ in (15 × 7cm) and the other 6 × 3½ in (15 × 9cm). On the larger piece, mark points 1 in (2.5cm) horizontally and 1⅜ in (3.5cm) vertically and cut out this corner rectangle. Fold under the paper by ⅝ in (15mm). Run the tracing wheel down this edge and again ⅝ in (15mm) from this line, parallel to the first line.

2 Turn the paper over and run the tracing wheel down from the top corner horizontally and vertically by 1⅜ in (3.5cm). Run the tracing wheel along the corner of the underside of the other rectangle, 1⅜ in (3.5cm) each way from the corner. Turn the paper the right way up and bend over the corners. Glue at both corners to form the collar and stick both pieces together.

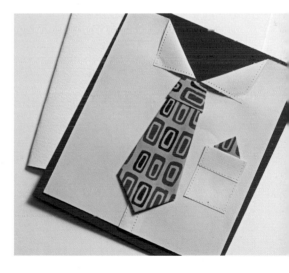

3 Cut out a rectangle of cream paper measuring 2¼ × 1¼ in (5.5 × 3cm) and fold over by ⅝ in (15mm). Run the tracing wheel along the edge of the cuff, down both sides, and across the bottom. Stick onto the shirt.

4 Using the templates on page 148, cut out the two pieces for the tie and the handkerchief piece from patterned paper. Fold the tie pieces where indicated and glue together. Glue in place on the shirt. Fold the handkerchief as indicated and glue into the top of the pocket.

5 Cut out a rectangle of colored card measuring 5½ × 6¼ in (14 × 16cm). Cut out a rectangle of cream card measuring 11¼ × 6½ in (28.4 × 16.4cm). Score down the center, 5⅝ in (14.2cm) from each side, and fold in half. Glue the red card onto this with glue stick and then stick the shirt and tie in place.

Ribbon and Bow Card

The stylish, elegant look of these cards belies the simplicity of the design. The success of the cards relies on the choice of the materials. Using beautiful gift-wrap and a selection of richly colored ribbons and braids, they couldn't be easier to create.

Materials

Thin, dark pink card

Patterned paper in rich colors

27in (68cm) of 1½-in (4-cm) wide satin ribbon

Two 9-in (23-cm) lengths of braid

Fast-drying, high-tack craft glue

Glue stick

Craft knife, cutting mat, and metal ruler

Pencil

Scissors

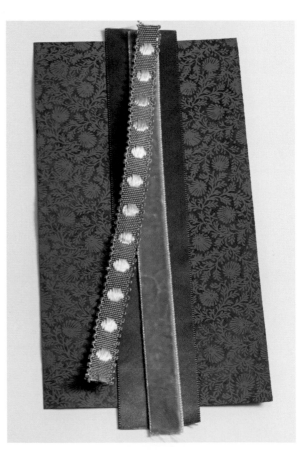

1 Cut out a rectangle of patterned paper measuring 8¼ x 4⅜ in (21 x 11 cm) using the craft knife, cutting mat, and metal ruler.

2 Cut a 9-in (23-cm) length of ribbon and stick horizontally across the patterned paper rectangle with glue stick, smoothing it as you go for a neat finish. There will be ½ in (1 cm) overhang at each end.

Tip
When adding a bow to the front of the cards, always glue a separate bow onto the flat ribbon rather than tie a bow with the ribbon on the card for a much neater finish.

3 Apply glue to the back of one of the lengths of braid and stick onto the satin ribbon band, again leaving ½ in (1 cm) overhang at each end.

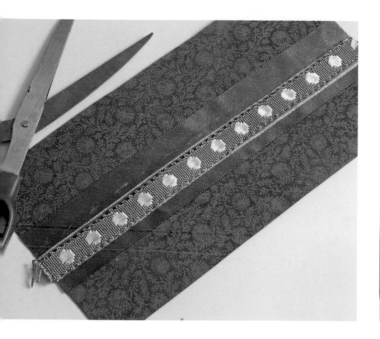

4 Glue the remaining length of braid on, smoothing it down to ensure a good adhesion. Trim the ends of the ribbon and braid with scissors as close to the paper as possible.

5 Tie a 18-in (45-cm) length of satin ribbon into a large bow. Cut the ends of the ribbon to even them up and stick to the front of the card. Cut a rectangle of dark pink card measuring 8¾ × 10in (22.5 × 25.5cm). Score down the center, 5in (12.75cm) from each side, and fold in half. Glue-stick the paper and ribbon part of the card to the front of the pink card.

Tissue Paper Card

Create a retro feel with a 1950s starburst motif.

The tissue paper colors are all of a similar hue, which adds to the effect. Use different sizes and colors to make a limitless number of designs. Overlapping different layers of tissue paper adds to the colorful effect and gives depth to the card.

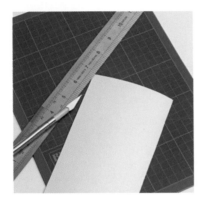

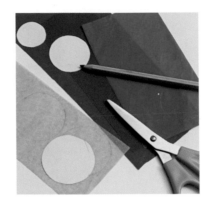

1 Cut out a rectangle of cream card measuring 4¼ x 7¼ in (10.5 x 18.5cm) using a craft knife and metal ruler.

2 Using the compass, draw three circles on scrap paper 2in (5cm), 1½ in (4cm), and 1 in (2.5cm) in diameter. Cut them out and draw around them onto tissue paper.

3 Cut out the tissue paper circles with scissors and make small "V" shaped snips all the way around them. Leave some of the smaller circles whole.

4 Arrange the cut and uncut tissue paper circles onto the cream card, moving them around until you have a pleasing arrangement. Lay some of the circles half on and half off the card.

5 Take one circle off the arrangement at a time and apply spray adhesive to one side of it. Stick it back in position. Continue until all the circles are stuck on. Trim the overhanging circles with scissors.

6 Cut out a 7¼ x 12½-in (18.5 x 32-cm) rectangle of red card. Score and fold in half. Stick a 7¼ x 5¼-in (18.5 x 13.5-cm) rectangle of orange paper onto the card, then stick the decorated panel onto this.

Materials

Thin card in red and
    cream
Orange paper
Tissue papers in red,
    orange, dark pink,
    and pale pink
Spray adhesive
Glue stick
Craft knife, cutting mat,
    and metal ruler
Compass and pencil

Tip

If you use glue stick
rather than spray
adhesive on the tissue
paper motifs, apply the
stick very gently to the
tissue paper to prevent
it tearing. Work from
the center of each
motif outward.

Spray-painted Fern Card

Spray paint is a very fast and effective way

of making several cards easily and simply. Choose strong colours for a contemporary look. Burnt orange, bright pink, and chocolate brown all work well together, or try different shades of green, in keeping with the leafy design. Any large leaves can be used, although it is better to avoid particularly delicate ones as these will be difficult to remove when covered in paint. Ferns and evergreen foliage are available all year round, or try seasonal shrubs and plants.

Materials

Thin card in blue and
    deep orange
Craft spray paint in
    brown and green
Spray adhesive
Fresh fern leaves, or
    similar
Craft knife, cutting mat,
    and metal ruler
Pencil
Scrap paper
Glue stick

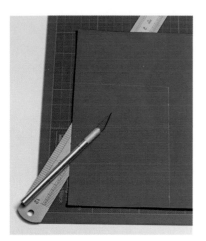

1 Using a pencil, draw a rectangle measuring 4⅜ × 5⅞in (11 × 15cm) on the card. Cut out using a craft knife, cutting mat, and metal ruler.

2 Working in a well-ventilated area and covering the worksurface completely with scrap paper, apply a thin coat of spray adhesive to the back of a fern leaf (it will be difficult to remove the leaf from the card in step 4 if too much adhesive is used).

3 Lay the leaf in position on the card and press down firmly. Don't worry if some parts of the leaf stick up slightly as this will create a pleasing, blurred effect. Working in a well-ventilated area on a covered surface, spray paint over the card and leaf in short bursts.

Tip

To make Christmas cards using this method, press branches of fir for a few days in a flower press or between some heavy books to flatten them. Try using white or silver spray paint for a wintery feel, adding berries of glitter glue or cut from shiny paper.

4 Carefully peel the leaf off the card before the paint dries completely, then leave the card to dry. Measure and cut out a 6¼ × 9½in (16 × 24cm) rectangle of the same colored card. Score gently down the center of the card and fold the card in half. Apply glue stick to the back of the decorated panel and stick it to the front of the card.

Embroidered Ribbon Bouquet Card

Make a truly special card using ribbon embroidery.

Thin silk ribbons in pastel colors are used with a traditional embroidery technique with a difference, as card is used instead of fabric. Embroider the whole bouquet design or make a smaller card with just a few flowers and leaves. Choose just one flower and embroider onto card for a gift tag as special as the actual gift. This card will take slightly longer to make than many of the other designs in this book, but a keepsake will be created and the time spent making it is sure to be much appreciated by the recipient.

Materials

1/8-in (3-mm) wide ribbon in pale pink, coral pink, pale blue, and green

Pale green embroidery thread

Embroidery needle

Scissors

Thin card in cream and other colors

Craft knife, cutting mat, and metal ruler

Pencil

1 Cut out a rectangle of cream card measuring 6 x 7in (15.25 x 18cm). Photocopy or trace the design for the embroidery on page 148. Using a light box or window, place the pattern behind the cream card and lightly trace over the pattern in pencil.

2 Cut a 16-in (40.5-cm) length of ribbon and thread it through the needle. Tie a double knot in the end and begin to stitch the flowers in the required position, starting from the back of the card.

3 Stitch the flowers in different colors, securing the end of the ribbon on the back of the card with a few back stitches. Make two stitches at the center of each flower. Trim the ends of the ribbon on the back of the card.

4 Using three strands of green embroidery thread and starting and finishing the thread on the back of the card, embroider lines of small stitches to create the flower stems.

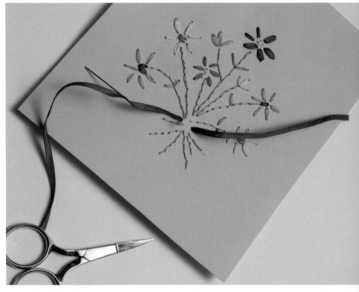

5 Using a short length of green ribbon, stitch a few leaves onto the flower stalks in the required positions.

6 Thread a 7-in (18-cm) length of pink ribbon through from the front of the card to the back and through to the front again, without a knot, and tie into a small bow. Trim the ends of the ribbon to the same length.

Tip
For a special finishing touch, embroider a flower and a few leaves onto a small rectangle of thin card and glue onto the front of the envelope to make a pretty label.

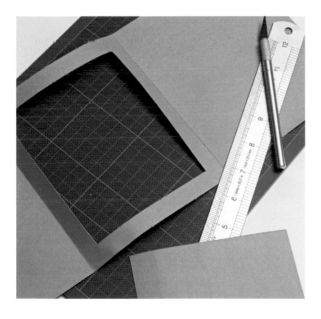

7 Cut a 6¼ x 16½-in (16 x 42-cm) piece of colored card. Mark and score the card into three even sections, all 5½ in (14cm) wide. Using a craft knife, cutting mat, and metal ruler, cut out a 4⅜ x 5-in (11 x 12.75-cm) rectangle from the center section.

8 Trim ¼ in (7mm) from each side of the embroidered panel using the craft knife and ruler, making the final size 5½ x 6½ in (14 x 16.4cm). Apply glue stick around the inside edge of the cutout rectangle and stick the embroidered panel face down onto this. Glue the left-hand panel of the card on top of this, pressing down firmly to ensure a good adhesion.

Metallic Leaf Card

Use a combination of silver, gold, and bronze metallic foils
to give a stunning stylish look. Size the card with adhesive, then lay the metallic leaf over
the top and brush gently with a soft bristled paintbrush to remove the excess leaf.

Materials

Thin, plum-colored card
Metallic leaf
Metallic leaf size
Fine paintbrush
Larger, dry paintbrush
Pencil
Craft knife, cutting mat, and
   metal ruler
24-in (60-cm) length of ⅛-in
   (3-mm) wide gold ribbon

1 Cut out a piece of card measuring 7½ × 8in (19 × 20.5cm). Score down the center, 4in (10.25cm) from each side, and fold neatly in half.

2 Measure and mark two squares, each measuring 2½ × 2½in (6 × 6cm), on the card faintly with pencil.

3 Using the smaller paintbrush, paint metallic leaf size onto both squares and leave to dry for 15 minutes.

4 Cut some gold leaf into a 2½-in (6-cm) square and lay it onto the top square. Repeat with silver leaf on the bottom square. Rub both squares over with a dry paintbrush to ensure a good adhesion and to remove any loose bits.

5 Tie the ribbon around the card, finishing with a bow. Trim the ends.

Tip

Store metallic leaf in a plastic bag, as the air will make it tarnish.

Blossom Hole-punch Card

The versatility of the hole punch is put to good use here, creating circles of paper which make these pretty flower blossoms. Punch holes in pastel-colored paper, then glue the circles together to form these delicate blossoms. For a more unusual look, the design is revealed when the two side flaps are opened.

Materials

Thin card in cream
    and bright pink
Paper in brown,
    pale pink, lilac,
    and pale green
Hole punch
Paper for the vase
Fast-drying, high-tack
    craft glue and a
    small pot
Toothpick
Glue stick
Craft knife, cutting mat,
    and metal ruler
Pencil

1 Punch holes in the pink and lilac papers, collecting the circles that are punched out. You will need about 54 circles in each color. Cut out nine small squares of paper in each color, about ¼in (7mm) square.

2 Stick six circles of paper in one color onto a square of paper, overlapping each one slightly, applying small dabs of glue to the backs of the circles with a toothpick. Continue until you have nine flowers in each color.

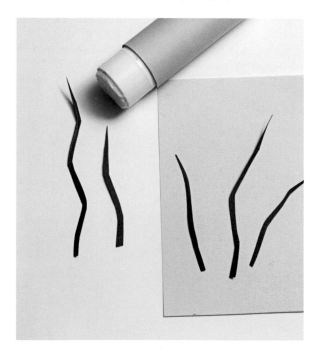

3 Cut out a rectangle of cream card measuring 5½ × 3¾in (14 × 9.5cm). Cut out branch shapes from brown paper and stick onto the cream card.

4 Arrange the flowers onto the branches, mixing up the colors, and glue in place with small dabs of craft glue applied with a toothpick.

5 Punch about 18 circles from the green paper and glue onto the branches between the flowers. Leave them slightly bent for a more three-dimensional look.

6 Cut a vase shape from brightly colored paper and glue in place. Cut a piece of bright pink card measuring 6 x 8in (15.25 x 20.5cm). Measure and mark a faint line 2in (5cm) in from each side and score along this line. Fold along the score lines and stick the decorated panel onto the middle section using glue stick.

Tip
A pretty alternative would be to make lots of the flower blossoms, arrange and glue them into a circular shape onto card to form a floral wreath.

Patchwork Card

Make a patchwork panel without sewing a stitch.

Cut small squares of fabrics, then decorate with hearts, using fusible webbing which will stop the fabrics fraying and stick them together. Lightweight cottons are the best materials to use for a neat finish. Floral designs will give a homespun, traditional look.

Materials

Scraps of fabric (about nine different fabrics)

Thin blue card

Plain pink fabric

Fusible webbing

Scissors

Craft knife, cutting mat, and metal ruler

Spray adhesive

Tip
Cut out simple flower shapes to decorate the patchwork squares instead of hearts, in keeping with the floral theme.

1 Using a medium-hot iron, iron fusible webbing onto the back of nine scraps of fabric, leaving the backing paper in position.

2 Draw a square measuring 1½ x 1½in (4 x 4cm) onto scrap paper to use as a template. Draw around the square onto the back of the fabric with a pencil, and cut out using scissors.

3 Copy the small heart template on page 149 and cut out (the larger heart can be used for a gift tag). Draw around the heart onto the back of the fabrics and cut out. You will now have nine squares and nine hearts. Arrange the hearts onto the squares. Peel the backing paper off the hearts, lay a damp cloth over the fabrics, and press carefully with a medium iron to fuse the hearts to the fabric squares.

4 Cut out a piece of plain pink fabric measuring 6¼ × 6¼ in (16 × 16cm). Peel the backing paper off the small squares, and lay the fabrics centrally onto the pink fabric, keeping the final arrangement in place. Ensure that the fabric squares butt up to each other, without leaving any gaps. Lay a damp cloth over the fabrics and press with a medium iron for a few seconds. Remove the damp cloth and press the fabrics again to dry them.

5 Trim the pink fabric by about ⅝ in (15mm) on each side, creating a ¼-in (7-mm) border all the way around the patchwork.

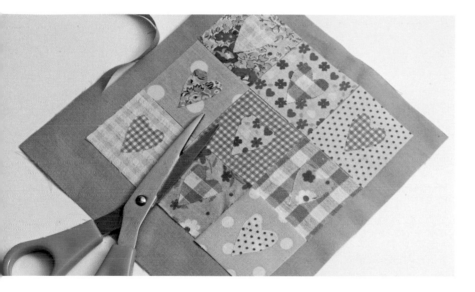

6 Cut a rectangle of blue card measuring 5½ × 11 in (14 × 28cm). Score down the center 5½ in (14cm) from each side and fold neatly in half. Working in a well-ventilated area, apply a fine coat of spray adhesive to the back of the patchwork panel and stick onto the front of the card, ensuring a flat finish.

Oak Leaf Card

Elegant and stylish, these charming oak leaf wreath cards can be made from a combination of different colored papers to suit any occasion. Use browns and oranges for an autumnal look, fresh greens for a springtime card, or try adding small red beads and buttons to look like berries for a more wintery theme.

Materials

Thin card in cream and brown or russet

Three co-ordinating shades of paper or thin card (greens or oranges and browns)

Craft knife, cutting mat, and metal ruler

Small, sharp scissors

Compass and pencil

Fast-drying, high-tack craft glue

Ribbon

1 Photocopy the oak leaf template on page 149 and cut out. Draw around the oak leaf onto the colored paper or thin card and cut out carefully with scissors. You will need about nine leaves in each color.

2 Cut out a 6-in (15.25-cm) square of cream card. Mark the center of the square faintly with a pencil and place the compass point on the mark. Draw a faint circle with a radius of 1¾in (4.5cm).

3 Arrange the leaves to form a wreath shape using the circle as a guide, applying a small dab of glue to the base of each one to secure it in place. Overlap the leaves slightly, leaving them slightly raised.

4 Cut a rectangle of colored card measuring 6¼ x 12½in (16 x 32cm). Score down the center, 6¼in (16cm) from each side, and fold neatly in half. Glue the wreath onto the backing card with glue stick.

5 Cut a 10-in (25.5-cm) length of ribbon and tie into a bow. Trim the ends and glue onto the wreath with craft glue.

Handbag Card

No outfit is complete without a handbag, and these fun cards fit the bill perfectly. Choose polka-dot and floral-patterned papers with a 1950s feel, and add pretty velvet and grosgrain ribbons to trim. Use a small Velcro patch so that the card can be opened and closed. Write your message and greetings inside the bag, and an envelope will not be needed.

Materials

Thin, pale colored card

Spotted and floral gift-wraps

Pale blue and bright pink
   tissue paper

¼-in (7-mm) and 1-in
   (2.5-cm) wide velvet
   ribbon in pale blue and
   bright pink

Craft knife, cutting mat,
   and metal ruler

Pencil

Scissors

Glue stick

Fast-drying, high-tack
   craft glue

Small Velcro pads

Tip

Instead of using Velcro, punch a hole in the bag and the flap and thread ribbon through, so it can be tied in a bow at the front.

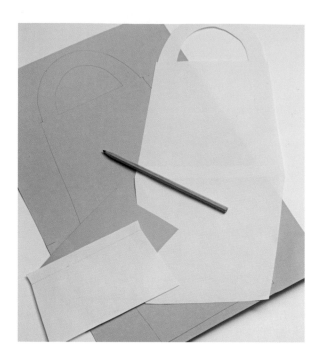

1 Photocopy the templates on page 149 and cut out. Draw around the bag shape and the front flap pieces on colored card and cut out with a craft knife.

2 Lay the two pieces onto gift-wrap and draw around them. Cut out and glue onto the card with glue stick. Cut out another handle shape and stick to the other side of the handle so both sides are covered in paper.

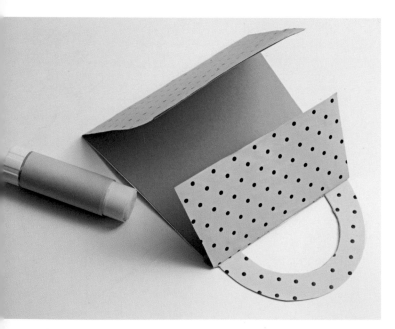

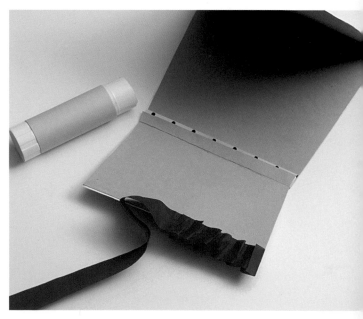

3 Score along the score line marked on the template on the plain card side of both pieces on the bag shape and front flap and bend them neatly. Stick the flap just underneath the handle with craft glue and hold in place until firmly stuck.

4 Cut a strip of tissue paper 16 x 1in (40.5 x 2.5cm). Apply a line of glue to the underside of the flap and stick the tissue paper to it, pleating it as you go. Press down firmly.

have a **MAGICAL** day

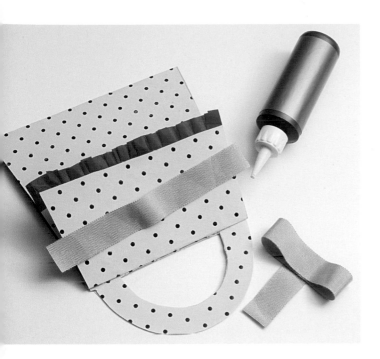

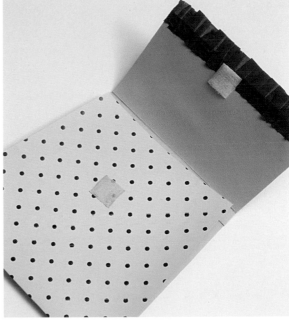

5 Glue a length of ribbon along the flap of the bag. Cut an 8-in (20.5-cm) length of grosgain ribbon. Make it into a loop with the join at the center of the back. Glue a 2½-in (6-cm) length of ribbon over the middle of this, holding it in place at the back with craft glue. Stick this onto a band of ribbon along the bottom edge of the flap.

6 Stick a small Velcro pad to the bag and inside of the flap to close the card.

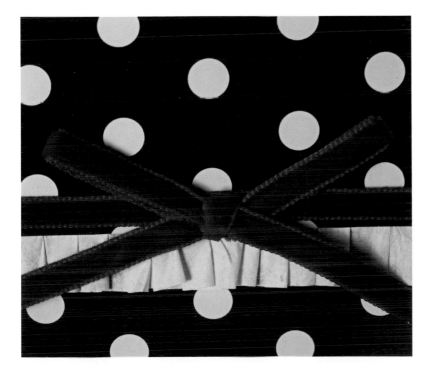

Paper Collage Flower Card

These simple flower shapes are joined together by brass paper fasteners. This bold and contemporary look using strong colors for the flowers is enhanced by a subtler background color. You can vary the designs of the flowers to add variety.

Materials

Colored card

Paper in pale pink, bright pink, red, pale blue, lilac, and green

Brass paperclips (four per card)

Scissors

Craft knife, cutting mat, and metal ruler

Glue stick

Pencil

Tip

For a neat finish, glue a piece of thin card inside the front of the greetings card to cover up the paper fasteners.

1 Photocopy the templates on page 150. You will need a large flower, a small flower, a center for the flowers, and a leaf shape. Cut these out and draw around them on colored papers. Cut them out neatly with scissors.

2 Cut out a rectangle of card measuring 8¼ × 12in (21 × 30.5cm). Score down the center, 6in (15.25cm) from each side, and fold in half.

3 Make an arrangement of flowers on the front of the card, using different colored flower parts and centers and adding green leaves randomly. Stick the small flowers and parts in place with glue stick.

4 Open up the card and make slits about ⅛in (7mm) wide at the center of each large flower. Push a paper clip through. Open up the clip on the inside of the card to secure in place.

Children's Cards

The cards featured in this chapter are full of color and character, and have been specially designed to appeal to children, either to make the greetings cards themselves with minimal adult supervision or to receive them. The Finger Puppet Card and the Peg Doll Card use only the simplest of sewing skills, and combine a gift within the design of the card, while the Felt Flower Card and Lollipop Card can easily be made by young children. The teabag folding technique featured on page 88 is quick to master, and the Corrugated Cards turn ordinary packing material into something special.

Finger Puppet Card

A greetings card and a present all in one,

these finger-puppet greetings are great fun for children. Using only simple stitches, they can be made by children as well as for them, and could even be entirely glued rather than sewn. Encourage them to make their own designs for the finger puppets, using favorite characters or animals and making scenes on the cards using paper collage and felt shapes.

Materials

A selection of felt in
    different colors
Embroidery thread
    and needle
Fast-drying, high-tack
    craft glue
Adhesive pads
Scissors
Wool for hair
Thin card in pastel
    colors

Tip

Sticky pads have been used to hold the puppets in place on each card, but you could also glue a paper pocket onto the front of the card, to sit the puppet in.

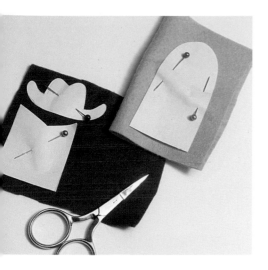

1 Photocopy the templates on page 150 and cut out all the pieces needed for each finger puppet in your chosen colors of felt.

2 Glue the clothes to the front piece of the puppet, using craft glue. Cut some short lengths of wool and glue in place as the hair. Leave to dry.

3 Using a short length of three strands of embroidery thread, tie a knot in the end and embroider simple crosses on the front of the puppet to represent the eyes. and, changing the color of thread, the mouth. Finish off on the wrong side with another knot.

4 Using three strands of embroidery thread and starting on the wrong side of the front of the puppet with a knot, stitch the front of the puppet to the back. Finish off with a knot inside the puppet.

5 Cut a piece of card measuring 6 x 8¼in (15.25 x 21cm); score and fold in half 4⅛in (10.5cm) from each edge. Using felt and the photocopied templates from page 150, cut out the background shapes for each puppet.

6 Stick the shapes onto the card using craft glue and leave to dry. Attach the finger puppet to the card with a sticky pad.

Lollipop Card

Good enough to eat, these fun cards are very easy to make and are suitable for any occasion, from birthday greetings to thank-you cards and party invitations. Because of the size of the lollipops, these cards are a great way to use up scraps of fabric. Try brightly colored polka-dot or floral fabrics for girls or stripes and checks for boys.

Materials

Thin card in cream and
    pastel colors
Bright fabrics in ginghams
    and polka dots
Light brown paper for the
    lolly sticks
Craft knife, cutting mat,
    and metal ruler
Spray adhesive
Glue stick
Scissors
Pencil

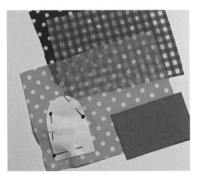

1 Photocopy the lollipop and stick shape templates on page 151. Cut the shapes out and use as templates to cut out fabric lollipops and brown paper sticks.

2 Cut a rectangle of cream card measuring 8½ × 6in (22 × 15.25cm). Measure and make a faint pencil mark down the center of the card, 3in (7.5cm) from each long side.

3 Apply spray adhesive to the back of the fabric lollipop shapes and stick onto the card, positioning roughly 1½in (4cm) of the lollipop shape below the central pencil line. Using the glue stick, glue the lollipop sticks in place.

4 Score along the pencil mark between the lollipops and at either end. Cut around the top of the lollipop shapes using a craft knife and cutting mat.

5 Cut a 8½ × 6¼-in (22 × 16-cm) rectangle of pastel card. Score a line centrally along the card, 3⅛in (8cm) in from each long side, and fold. Glue this card to the back of the lollipops with glue stick, to make the card stand up.

Felt Flower Card

Simple felt flowers make these attractive celebratory cards, with a bright sequin used as the centerpiece. Choose felt in strong colors, using clashing colors together for a cheery and bright look. Children may need help cutting the felt flowers out, but making the rest of the card is very simple and will require minimum adult intervention.

Materials

Thin cream card

Plain colored paper

Felt in bright colors (including green for the leaves)

5½-in (14-cm) length of ⅛-in (3-mm) wide green ribbon

Two large sequins

Fast-drying, high-tack craft glue

Glue stick

Craft knife, cutting mat, and metal ruler

Pencil

Scissors

1 Photocopy the flower templates and the leaf from page 151 and use them as pattern pieces on the felt. Cut out two large flowers and two small flowers in different colors, and three green felt leaves.

2 Stick the small flower to the center of the large flower, and glue a sequin to the center of this. Allow to dry.

3 Cut out a rectangle of cream card measuring 6¼ × 12¼ in (16 × 31cm). Score down the center of the card 6⅛ in (15.5cm) in from each long side, and fold.

4 Cut out a rectangle of plain colored paper measuring 6⅛ × 6¼ in (15.5 × 16cm). Stick onto the front of the cream card with glue stick.

5 Glue the flowers onto the card with craft glue, positioning one higher than the other. Glue lengths of ribbon onto the card as flower stems. Glue the leaves in place.

Peg Doll Card

$\mathcal{O}$ld-fashioned dolly pegs or clothes pins are transformed into these delightful greetings cards that are perfect for young girls. A huge array of characters can be created using scraps of fabrics, oddments of braid, and pieces of ribbon. The attractive box houses the peg doll to create a card which becomes a gift in itself.

Materials

Dolly peg or old-fashioned clothes pin

Felt-tipped pens in pink, brown, green, and blue

Embroidery thread for the hair

Scraps of fabric for the dress

Glitter

Ribbon and little jewels or beads to decorate

Fast-drying, high-tack craft glue

Patterned gift wrap

Thin colored card

Needle and thread

Scissors

Rotary hole punch

Craft knife, cutting mat, and metal ruler

Pencil

1 Using the felt-tipped pens, draw a face onto the head of the clothes pin. Practice drawing the features on paper first if necessary.

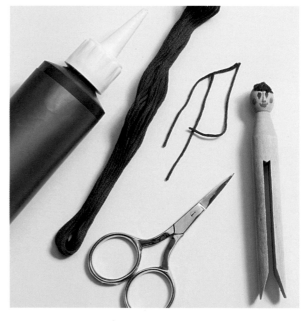

2 Glue about four pieces of embroidery thread, each about ¼in (7mm long), above the face to form the hair, using craft glue. Cut six or seven lengths of embroidery thread, each about 1½in (4cm) long, and glue over the top of the head. When dry, trim the ends to the same length.

84

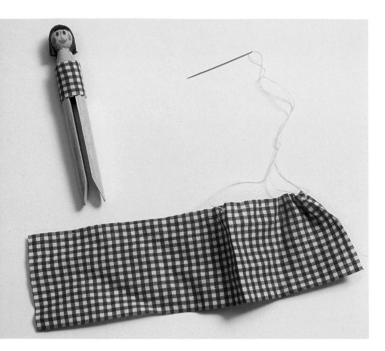

3 Cut out a piece of fabric measuring 1¾ × 2in (4.5 × 5cm), fold in half widthways, 1in (2.5cm) from each side, and glue onto the peg to form the bodice of the dress. Cut out a rectangle of fabric measuring 2¼ × 8in (5.5 × 20.5cm) for the skirt. Using the needle and thread, make a running stitch along the top of the fabric and gather slightly to fit around the peg, finishing with a few stitches to hold in place at the end. Glue onto the clothes pin.

Tip
Theme your card's character by modeling the peg doll on the recipient, or alternatively decorate for specific occasions such as Easter or Christmas.

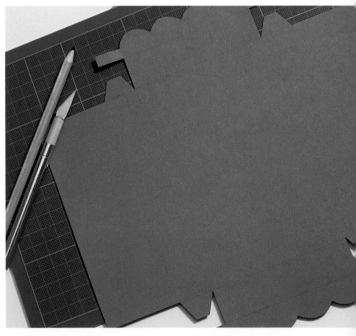

4 Glue a 2-in (5-cm) length of ribbon around the waist of the dress. Stick a bow at the top of the dress or on the hair, adding a few jewels or beads to decorate. Apply a little glue to the "feet" and dip in glitter to form the shoes.

5 Using the template on page 151, measure and draw out a card piece to make the box. Cut out the box shape carefully with the craft knife and metal ruler. Score where indicated.

6 Punch holes in the scalloped edge using a small setting on the rotary hole punch.

7 Glue the card box together using craft glue, holding each section in place until dry. Punch holes on the two doors.

8 Cut out a rectangle of patterned paper measuring 4 x 6in (10 x 15.25cm) and glue onto the back of the inside of the box with glue stick. Cut out two rectangles of paper measuring 2 x 6in (5 x 15.25cm) and glue them onto the inside of the doors.

9 Cut two small, central slits in the back of the box, thread a piece of ribbon through the slits, and tie around the doll, finishing with a bow. Thread two lengths of ribbon through the holes in the doors, and tie together to close the card.

Teabag-folding Flower Card

These pretty floral cards are made using the popular technique originally devised to fold teabag envelopes. Here, used with plain papers, the basic folds are used to create a simple but unusual flower motif, finished off with ribbon and a button, with folded paper triangle leaves. The folding method used is deceptively simple, and once mastered, making a flower takes no time at all.

Materials

Thin paper in pinks and greens

Thin card for backing in pinks and pale blue

Pearl buttons, ½in (1cm) in diameter

⅛-in (3-mm) wide green satin ribbon, about 4⅜in (11cm) for each card

Fast-drying, high-tack craft glue

Scissors

Craft knife, cutting mat, and metal ruler

Glue stick

Tip

The same folded triangle could be used to create all sorts of patterns, and by using patterned papers, an array of finishes can be achieved.

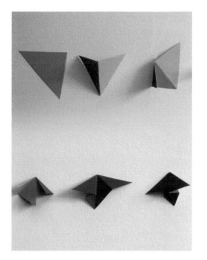

1 Cut out four squares measuring 1½ × 1½ in (4 × 4cm) from the thin paper. On each square, draw a line from one corner to the opposite corner and cut across it to form two triangles.

2 Take a triangle and fold in half, wrong sides together. Open out again. Lay wrong side down, fold the top points down to the bottom fold line. Open out again. With right sides together, fold the right-hand and left-hand fold lines to the central fold, and crease. Repeat with all eight triangles.

3 Glue the paper petals together to form a flower shape, following the photograph.

4 Cut out a rectangle of card measuring 6¼ × 4in (16 × 10cm). Glue a length of green ribbon onto the card to form a stalk. Glue the paper flower to the top of this.

5 Glue a button to the center of the flower. Make two leaves using the green paper following the steps above and glue onto each side of the stalk.

6 Cut out a rectangle of co-ordinating colored card measuring 8½ × 6½ in (22 × 17cm). Fold in half. Glue the card front to this with glue stick and press down firmly.

Raffia Card

Make these bright and cheery woven raffia cards

for a birthday or just to say thank-you to friends and family. They are so quick and easy to make that a whole collection can be made in an afternoon, with gift tags and envelopes to match. Finish off with a fun tassel on the envelope for an unusual detail.

Materials

Thin, brightly colored card

Thin corrugated cardboard

Colored raffia

Rotary hole punch

Pencil and scrap paper

Scissors

Craft knife, cutting mat, and
    metal ruler

Embroidery needle

Fast-drying, high-tack craft glue

Tip

Try using the colored corrugated card and different colors of raffia, now widely available, and make small gift tags using a simple circle motif.

1 Using the heart template on page 149 and the star template on page 156, cut out a heart and star shape using scrap paper. Lay the corrugated cardboard textured side down and draw around the templates. Cut out the shapes with scissors.

2 In pencil, mark the position for the holes using the template. Using the smallest hole punch setting, make a hole at each mark.

3 Take a strand of raffia and thread it through the needle. Stitch the raffia through the holes on the cardboard shapes, securing the ends with a dab of glue on the back.

4 Cut out a rectangle of colored card measuring 11 × 5½ in (28 × 12.75cm). Score along the halfway mark and fold in half. Glue the woven corrugated shapes firmly onto the front of the card, holding in place until well adhered.

5 To make a tassel, cut a piece of cardboard about 2¾ in (7cm) wide (the length doesn't matter). Wind a double length of raffia around the card and thread a piece measuring about 6in (15.25cm) in length underneath the raffia.

6 Tie the short length of raffia at what will be the top of the tassel with a tight knot. Cut along the bottom of the raffia and remove from the cardboard. Tie another length of raffia ⅝ in (15mm) from the top of the tassel, securing with a knot. Trim the ends neatly.

Special Occasions

There are certain events in life that deserve to be marked with a unique, handmade card—the arrival of a new baby, an engagement or wedding, the first Valentine's day shared with a loved one, or moving into a new home. This chapter provides a host of beautiful cards to celebrate these special milestones, plus plenty of ideas for celebrating other traditional occasions, including Thanksgiving, Easter, and Mother's Day. The designs range from fun, pop-up cards to stylish pin-pricked patterns, and also include designs which can be produced in bulk for Christmas.

Quilled Valentine Card

$\mathcal{S}$how your true love how you really feel with a beautifully handcrafted valentine card. Quilling, in its simplest form, is the art of forming intricate patterns using thin strips of paper and can be used to make elegant hearts and scrolls, as well as many other shapes. Join coils of paper together to form a border around the card and decorate with hearts and other simple designs. Although relatively simple to master, quilling is quite time-consuming, so put aside plenty of time and enjoy using this traditional craft to make a very personal and individual card.

Materials
Cream or white quilling
    paper, ¼in (7mm)
    wide
Thin card in red and
    white
Craft knife, cutting mat,
    and metal ruler
Pencil
Fast-drying, high-tack
    craft glue
Toothpick

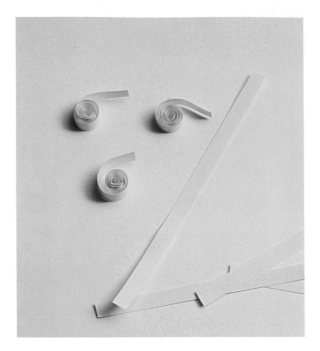

1 Take the quilling paper and cut 4in (10cm) lengths. Carefully curl each strip and roll up to make a coil. Let go of the coil. Continue to make paper coils, trying to make them all the same size.

2 Cut a rectangle of red card measuring 4⅜ × 6in (11 × 15.25cm). Glue paper coils around the rectangle to create a border, applying small dabs of glue with a toothpick. Glue the end of each coil to the next one.

Tip
Use this technique to make gift tags with one simple heart in the middle and a few scrolls stuck around it to form a border.

3 Cut lengths of quilling paper about 4¾ in (12cm) long. Fold in half, open out slightly and curl both ends inward to make a heart shape. Glue together, using dabs of glue on a toothpick, so the heart holds its shape. Make four hearts and glue inside the coiled border on the red card.

4 Cut four lengths of quilling paper about 4in (10cm) long. Fold them in half and coil the ends outward. Glue from the fold about ¾in (2cm) and hold in place until dry. Glue these shapes between the heart shapes.

5 Cut out a rectangle of white card measuring 9½ × 6¼in (24 × 16cm). Fold in half, scoring along the fold line to create a neat finish. Glue the quilled part of the card to this.

Heart Card

Delight your valentine with this simple but effective card from the heart. Use a heart-shaped hole punch on squares of paper in strong, passionate pinks, oranges, and reds, and set out them in a neat panel for a bold, contemporary look.

Materials

Thin card in cream, bright pink, red, burnt orange, burgundy, and deep pink
Heart-shaped hole punch
Craft knife, cutting mat, and metal ruler
Pencil
Glue stick

Tip

Try to use lightweight paper and card with the hole punch as thicker card will not produce such a clean cut.

1 Cut out eight squares of card, two of each color, each measuring 1½ x 1½in (4 x 4cm), using the craft knife and metal ruler.

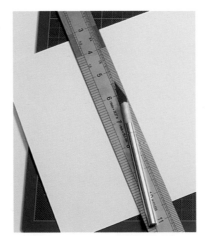

2 Mark a pencil dot in the center of each square and punch a hole in each, using this pencil mark as your guide.

3 Cut out a rectangle of cream card measuring 7 x 8in (18 x 20cm). Score a line down the center of the card, 4in (10cm) from each side, and fold in half.

4 Arrange the heart-punched squares onto the front of the card and glue in place with glue stick.

Doily Card

Paper doilies don't have to be just for cake stands.

These pretty engagement cards use doilies in a completely different way. Cut them up and make new patterns with them, gluing small shapes in straight lines to make delicate borders and using flower and leaf motifs as central decorations.

Materials

Thin cream card

Paper in pale pink and
    pale lilac

Paper doilies

Compass and pencil

Craft knife, cutting mat,
    and metal ruler

Scissors

Glue stick

1 Cut out a 6¼-in (16-cm) square of lilac paper and a 5¼-in (13.5-cm) square of pink paper. Using the compass, draw and cut out a circle with a diameter of 4⅜ in (11cm) in lilac paper.

2 Take the doilies and cut out small sections to use on the card. Pick out parts of the border that may not be the correct shape but can be cut up and re-arranged.

3 Stick small shapes to the back of the pink square with glue stick to form a neat edging. Glue onto the lilac square when finished.

Tip
Make sure you have enough of each doily decoration when making borders. You may need several of the same doily for some patterns.

4 Glue shapes around the circle, again gluing them around the back, and stick onto the pink paper square.

5 Glue more doily decorations onto the circle in a pleasing arrangement.

6 Cut out a rectangle of cream card measuring 6½ × 13½in (17 × 34cm). Score down the center 6¾in (17cm) in from each long side and fold in half. Stick the decorated panel in place.

Lavender Heart Card

For a Mother's Day card that is both attractive and fragrant, make a lavender-filled heart. This simple card makes for a truly heart-warming greeting, and has the additional benefit that the heart can be removed and slipped into a drawer to scent linens. Use scraps of pretty cotton fabrics to make the heart and to stick onto the card as a background, and add a ribbon bow to complete the look.

Materials

Scraps of pretty fabric
  (two different ones
  for each card)
Thin card in cream
  and pink
Dried lavender
8-in (20.5-cm) length
  of ⅝-in (15-mm)
  wide ribbon
Spray adhesive
Craft knife, cutting mat,
  and metal ruler
Sewing machine
Pins, needle, and thread
Pinking shears
Scrap paper
Glue stick
Sticky pads

1 Using the template on page 152, cut out a heart from paper and pin to a double thickness of fabric. Cut out the heart and remove the pattern and pins.

2 Pin the hearts together, wrong sides facing, and machine stitch ½in (1cm) from the edge, leaving a gap of about 1¼in (3cm) along one side.

Tip
The fabric heart could be filled with any scented seeds or dried flowers. Try dried rose petals or pot pourri for an alternative fragrance.

3 Roll a piece of scrap paper up to make a funnel and fill the heart with dried lavender through the gap in the stitching. Machine stitch the opening closed.

4 Cut around the heart with pinking shears close to the stitching line to make a pretty edging. Hand stitch a ribbon bow onto the heart.

5 Cut out a rectangle of pink card measuring 5½ × 6¼in (14 × 16cm). Cut out a rectangle of co-ordinating fabric measuring 5 × 5⅞in (13 × 15cm). Working in a well-ventilated area, apply spray adhesive to the back of the fabric, and stick onto the pink card.

6 Cut out a rectangle of cream card measuring 6¾ × 12¼in (17 × 31cm). Score down the center of the card 6⅛in (15.5cm) in from each long side and fold over. Stick the pink card onto this with glue stick. Put a sticky pad onto the center of the card and stick the heart in place.

Pin-hole Card

Make your own pin-hole tool to make this hole-punched card perfect for an engagement. Simply push the eye of a large needle into a cork and use as a handle to protect your hand when punching holes into paper. The pattern is drawn onto paper and the holes are punched accordingly, to create a pretty, pin-hole effect design.

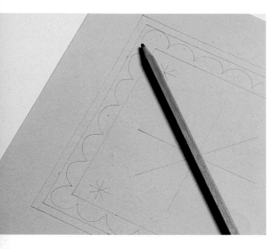

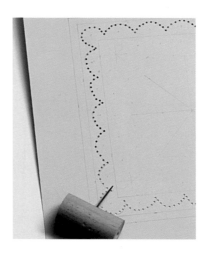

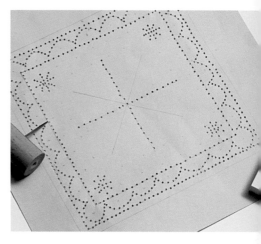

1 Photocopy the template on page 153. Cut out an 8½-in (22-cm) square of blue paper. Place this on top of the photocopy on a light box or stick to a window; lightly trace the pattern onto the paper with a pencil.

2 Using the cork with a needle pushed into it, start to punch holes along the pencil lines ⅛ in (3mm) apart, holding the paper away from the surface so that the needle will go right through it.

3 Continue to punch holes along all the pencil lines and where indicated on the template until the whole pattern is covered. Carefully rub out all the pencil lines with an eraser.

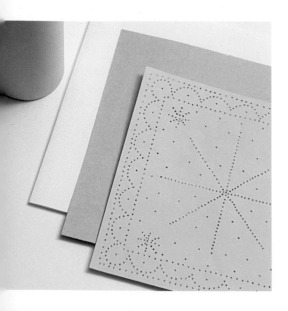

4 Trim 1⅜ in (3.5cm) from all sides of the patterned paper to make a neat edge. Cut a 6¼-in (16-cm) square of blue card and a rectangle of cream card measuring 6¾ x 13½ in (17 x 34cm). Score a line down the center of the card lengthways and fold. Apply spray adhesive to the back of the blue card and stick onto the cream card. Repeat with the patterned paper and stick centrally onto the blue card.

Tip
When gluing the hole-punched paper onto the backing card, do not press down too hard on it otherwise the pattern will lose its clarity.

Materials

Thin card in cream
and blue
Pale blue paper
Cork with the eye of
a needle pushed
into it
Pencil
Craft knife, cutting mat,
and metal ruler
Eraser
Spray adhesive

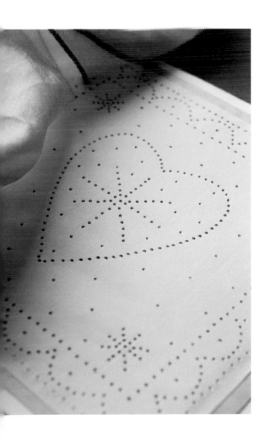

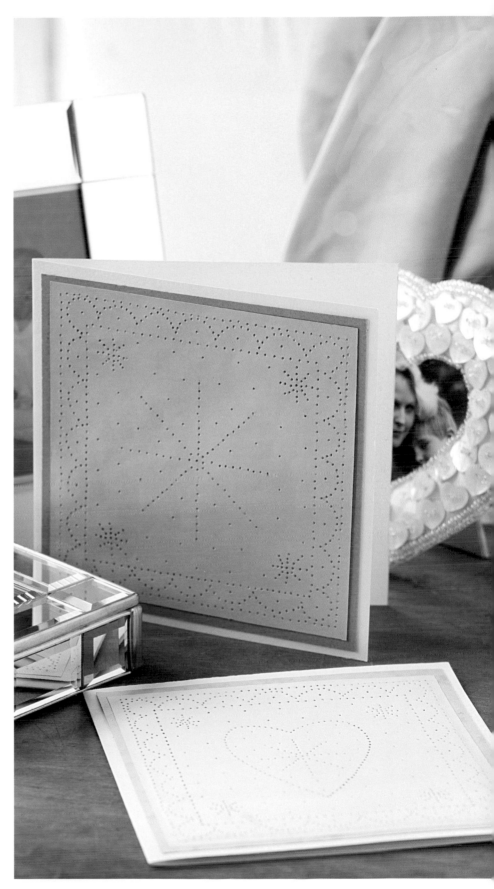

Wedding Cake Card

Delicate papers, tiny pearl buttons, and pretty braid create a beautifully elegant tiered wedding cake card that is as special as the day it commemorates. Use subtle shades of gray and silver for a stylish and sophisticated look, or choose brighter colors for a more contemporary feel.

Materials

Thin card in cream and gray

Five different patterned papers

Silver paper

Selection of silver braids and
    small buttons

Ribbon

Craft knife, cutting mat, and
    metal ruler

Scissors

Glue stick

Fast-drying, high tack craft glue

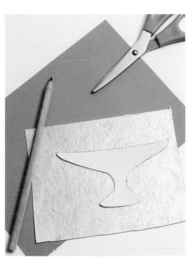

1 Cut out a rectangle of gray card measuring 8¼ x 5¾ in (21 x 14.5cm). Photocopy the templates from page 152 and cut out. Draw around the cake stand shape on silver paper, cut out with scissors, and glue-stick onto the gray card.

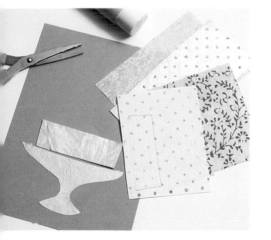

2 Using the templates, cut out the cake layers, using a different paper for each one. Arrange these above the cake stand on the card background and glue in place with glue stick.

3 Cut out a rectangle of cream card measuring 8¾ x 12½ in (22.5 x 32cm). Score down the center, 6¼ in (16cm) in from each long edge and fold in half. Glue the decorated front of the card to this using glue stick.

4 Cut lengths of braid and arrange onto the lower edges of the cake tiers, adding small buttons as well. When you are happy with the positioning, glue them in place using craft glue. Add a small bow to the cake stand, gluing it firmly in place.

Pop-up Wedding Present Card

These pop-up cards are gifts in themselves.
Use subtle colours and beautifully delicate patterned papers to create
these stylish and elegant wedding cards. Keep the design simple using
just one or two presents or create a more extravagant look with a big
pile of boxed gifts, topped off with a pretty bow.

Materials

Thin card in cream and
  soft brown
Co-ordinating patterned
  and plain wrapping
  papers
20in (51cm) of ½-in
  (1-cm) wide ribbon

Craft knife, cutting mat,
  and metal ruler
Glue stick
Fast-drying, high-tack
  craft glue
Scallop-bladed scissors
Pencil

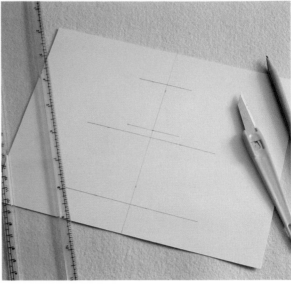

1 Cut out a rectangle of cream card measuring 8½ × 7¼ in (22 × 18.5cm). Draw a line ¼ in (5mm) in from the edges. Cut along this line with the shaped scissors.

2 Draw a line down the center of the card and score along it gently.

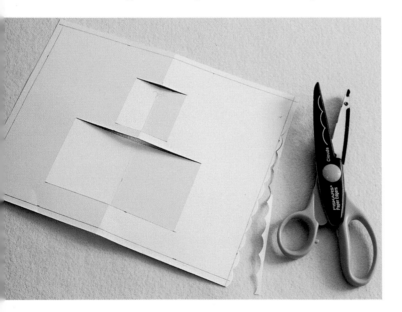

3 Measure and mark a line centrally 4⅜ in (11cm) long, 1¼ in (3cm) from the bottom of the card. Mark another line parallel to this, 2½ in (6cm) above it, also 4⅜ in (11cm) long. Draw another line ¼ in (7mm) from this line, again centrally, 2¾ in (7cm) long and another one the same length 2in (5cm) above it. Cut along these lines with a craft knife. Fold the card in half along the fold line, pushing the present sections the opposite way to the main fold.

4 Cut out a rectangle of patterned paper measuring 4⅜ × 2½ in (11 × 6cm) and a rectangle of plain paper measuring 2¾ × 1¾ in (7 × 4.5cm). Fold these both in half and apply glue to the back of them. Glue onto the present shapes on the card, pressing down firmly.

5 Cut two lengths of ribbon for each present about ¾ in (2cm) longer than the height of the present. Glue onto the presents, tucking the ends over to the back of the presents and securing with a dab of glue.

6 Cut a length of ribbon about 8in (20.5cm) long and tie into a bow. Cut out a piece of brown card measuring 9 x 6¾ in (23 x 17cm). Score gently along the center and fold in half. Glue the front of the card to the back. Glue the bow to the top of the present.

Tip
Make a gift tag using a square of card and a piece of patterned paper stuck to one side. Glue ribbon onto it and attach to the present with a bow.

New Baby Card

Bands of pretty pink and blue gingham ribbons have been used to great effect here to create these charming cards to celebrate the arrival of a new baby. Keep to the traditional shades of pink for a girl and blue for a boy, or create a more unisex look using a mixture of pastel colors. Simple and quick to make, these ribbon cards could be made to suit any number of occasions.

Materials

Thin card in blue and white
Selection of ribbons
High-tack, fast-drying craft glue
Scissors
Craft knife, cutting mat, and
    metal ruler

1 Cut out a rectangle of blue card measuring 6¼ x 5⅞in (16 x 15cm). Cut lengths of ribbon about 7in (18cm) long.

2 Lay the strips of ribbon over the card, moving them around until you are happy with the arrangement. Glue the ribbons onto the card, leaving about ⅝in (15mm) overhanging at each end. Ensure the ribbons are straight on the card. Vary the widths of the gaps between the ribbons.

3 Turn the card over and glue the ends of the ribbons to the back, ensuring that they are well stuck down.

4 Cut out a rectangle of white card measuring 12½ x 7in (32 x 18cm). Gently score a line with the craft knife along the center of the card, 6¼in (16cm) from each end. Fold the card in half. Apply glue to the back of the ribbon card and stick centrally onto the folded card.

5 Choose three ribbons that have been used on the card and cut an 8-in (20.5-cm) length of each. Tie them into bows and glue securely onto the corresponding ribbon on the card.

Tip
Use this design to make Easter cards using ribbons in shades of yellow, or a Mother's Day card made with some beautifully patterned ribbons in shades of lilac and lavender.

Easter Egg Card

Quick to make and very effective, these Easter egg cards will delight adults and children alike. Collect gift-wrap in polka dots and pretty patterns to make the egg shapes, and decorate with rickrack braid and ribbons in pastel colors. Use just one large egg on each card or stick two or three smaller ones in a line for a variation.

Materials

Thin card in cream and pastel colors

Spotted gift wrap

Chunky rickrack braid

Pastel-colored ribbon

Craft knife, cutting mat, and metal ruler

Pencil

Scissors

Glue stick

Fast-drying, high-tack craft glue

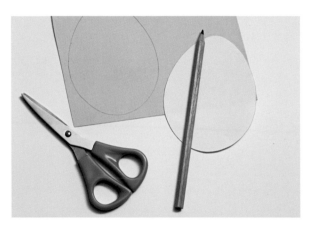

1 Photocopy the egg template on page 154 and cut out. Draw around the template onto pastel colored card and cut out neatly.

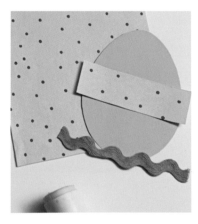

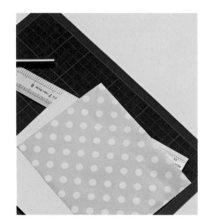

2 Cut a 1¼ x 3¾-in (3 x 9.5-cm) strip of spotted paper. Apply glue stick to the back and stick it across the egg; trim the ends. Cut a 4⅜-in (11-cm) length of rickrack; glue it across the egg, turning the ends to the back and gluing in place.

3 Cut out a 4¾ x 6¼-in (12 x 16-cm) rectangle of spotted paper. Cut out a 13½ x 5½-in (34 x 13.5-cm) rectangle of cream card; score and fold in half lengthways. Glue-stick the spotted paper to the front of the card.

4 Using glue stick, glue the egg to the center of the card. Cut a 12-in (30.5-cm) length of co-ordinating ribbon and tie in a bow. Glue the bow to the top of the egg with a dab of craft glue.

Easter Basket Card

Give a pretty basket filled with eggs for an unusual Easter greeting. The basket is made from strips of paper woven together to create texture. Finish the basket with a trim along the top and bottom, cut using scissors with shaped blades, and a large bow. Fill the basket with eggs cut from pretty pastel papers in varying sizes, and add a strip of tissue paper "grass" for a card worthy of any Easter egg hunt.

Materials

Thin card in lavender, cream, and pale yellow

Pastel colored papers for the eggs

Shaped scissors

Craft knife, cutting mat, and metal ruler

Pencil

Scissors

11in (28cm) length of pink ribbon, 1in (2.5cm) wide

Green tissue paper

Glue stick

Scrap paper

Tip

Make the basket with brown paper and cut pumpkin shapes from orange papers instead of eggs to make the card suitable for a Thanksgiving greeting.

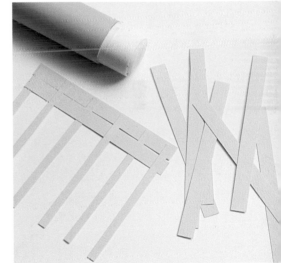

1 Measure and cut nine strips of yellow card, each ½ x 4⅜ in (1 x 11cm). Cut out six strips of yellow card, each ¼ x 3½ in (7mm x 9cm).

2 Lay one of the wider strips horizontally on the table. Stick the ends of all six thin strips to this with glue stick so that the strips lie vertically, ⅝in (15mm) apart.

3 Glue the end of a wide strip to the thin strip on the far left and weave the rest of the strip through the vertical strips. Make sure that this strip butts up to the strip along the top. Glue the other end to the vertical strip on the far right.

119

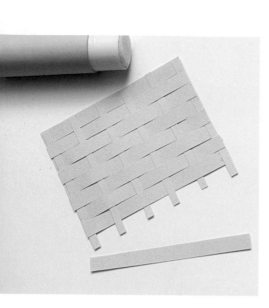

4 Glue another wide strip to the underside of the vertical strip on the far left, butting it up to the previous strip again, and weave as above. Glue the end in place on the far right. Continue until all the thick strips have been woven, remembering to alternate going under and over the strips to form a basketweave. Ensure that all the ends are firmly glued in place.

5 Apply glue stick to the back of the woven panel and stick onto some scrap paper. Using the basket shape template on page 154, draw the basket onto the woven panel and cut out with scissors.

6 Dab glue onto any ends of the strips that are not stuck down. Cut out a strip of yellow card using the shaped scissors, about ½ in (1cm) wide and long enough to trim the top and bottom of the basket. Glue in place.

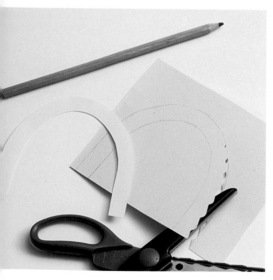

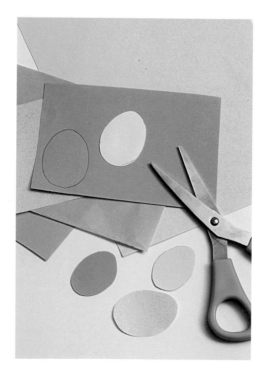

7 Cut out a handle using the template on page 154 and shaped scissors so it resembles basketwork.

8 Cut a 6 × 8½-in (15.25 × 22-cm) rectangle of cream card. Using the egg templates on page 154, cut out about seven paper eggs in a variety of colors.

9 Glue the basket handle onto the cream card and press down firmly. Arrange the paper eggs on the card and glue in place.

10 Cut a strip of green tissue paper 4⅜in (11cm) long and ¾in (2cm) wide. Make "V" shaped snips about two-thirds through the width of the tissue paper to look like grass, and stick along the bottom of the eggs.

11 Glue the basket shape in place, ensuring it is well stuck down. Tie a neat bow with the ribbon and stick onto the top of the basket.

12 Cut a 9 x 12½ in (23 x 32-cm) rectangle of lavender card. Score down the center, 6¼in (16cm) from each side and fold. Glue the front of the card onto this.

Pumpkin Card

Perfect for a Thanksgiving greeting or Halloween party invitation, these fun pumpkin cards are machine stitched to create an unusual effect. Choose lightweight papers in oranges and soft browns, cut them into pumpkin shapes, and stitch them onto card. It doesn't matter if the stitching is a little uneven as some irregularity will add to the charm.

Materials

Thin card in orange and cream

Brown craft paper

Paper in three shades of orange

Matching orange thread

Sewing machine

Scissors

Green paper

Green thread

Glue stick

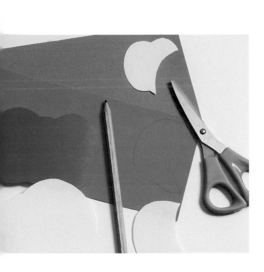

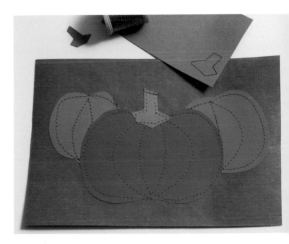

1 Using the templates on page 155, photocopy the pumpkin shapes and stalks and cut out. Lay the shapes onto the orange papers, draw around them, and cut out with scissors.

2 Cut out a rectangle of brown craft paper measuring 7½ × 5¼in (19 × 13cm) using a craft knife and metal ruler. Lay the pumpkins in the middle of the paper and hold in place with a dab of glue stick on the back. Machine stitch in place.

3 Cut out three green stalks and machine stitch them onto the pumpkins using green thread.

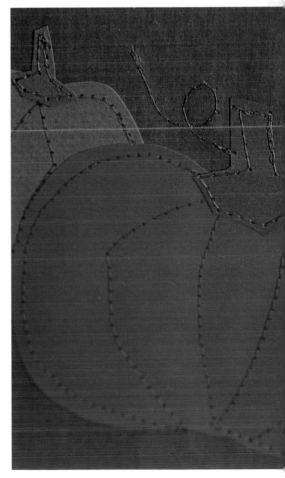

4 Draw some tendrils at the top of the big pumpkin faintly with a pencil and machine stitch along the lines with green thread.

Tip
Stitch a small pumpkin shape onto a square of card and use as a matching gift tag.

5 Cut out a rectangle of cream card measuring 8 × 5½in (20.5 × 14cm) and a rectangle of orange card measuring 8¼ × 12in (21 × 30.5cm). Score a line down the center of the orange card 6in (15.25cm) from each side; fold in half. Glue the cream card onto the orange card with the fold at the top; glue the pumpkins onto this, with an even border all around.

Rubber Stamp Leaf Card

Create these autumnal leaf cards, ideal for Thanksgiving, with a shop-bought rubber stamp. Stamping is a very effective method of producing multiple greetings cards very quickly, and can be used on any size or shape of card. Choose three or four different colors of ink pads and stamp randomly all over the card, placing the stamp off the edge of the card in places to create half leaves, to fill the space evenly.

Tip
Take sheets of plain paper and stamp randomly with different colored leaves to make an unusual gift-wrap.

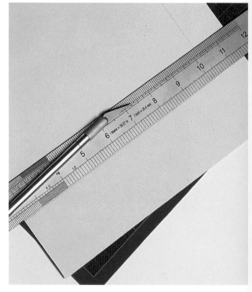

Materials
Thin card in deep orange and cream

Rubber stamp in a leaf shape

Ink pads in four colors

Craft knife, cutting mat, and metal ruler

Scrap paper

Glue stick

1 Cut out a rectangle of cream card measuring 6 x 8in (15.25 x 20.5cm), using a craft knife and metal ruler.

2 Try out a leafy pattern on scrap paper, then begin stamping on the card with one color, rocking the stamp slightly to ensure it makes even contact with the paper. Re-apply the ink after each stamp to keep an even density of the color.

3 Continue to stamp with the remaining colors, stamping on scrap paper a few times between colors to clean the stamp.

4 Cut a backing card measuring 8¼ × 12in (21 × 30.5cm). Score down the center, 6in (15.25cm) from each side, and fold in half. Glue the decorated panel onto this card with the fold at the top, using glue stick.

Button Christmas Card

When making Christmas cards, simple designs work best as you often need to make a large quantity of cards. Take a basic triangle shape cut from craft paper and raid your sewing basket for braid, buttons, and beads. Apple green and pale blue teamed with pink and red have been used to good effect here for a modern festive feel.

Materials

Thin card in cream and red

Craft paper in pale blue and green

Patterned paper

Selection of rickrack, buttons, and bobble braid

Star-shaped button

Craft knife, cutting mat, and metal ruler

Glue stick

Fast-drying, high-tack craft glue

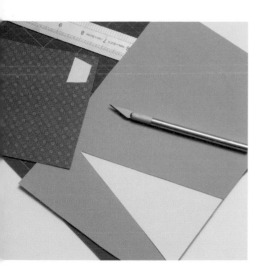

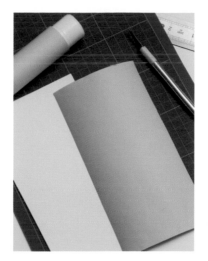

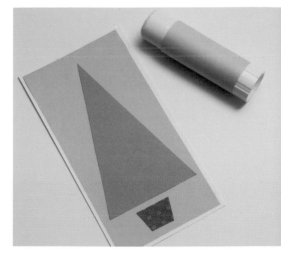

1 Photocopy the tree templates and base from page 155 and cut out the shapes. Draw around the templates on the green paper for the trees and on the patterned paper for the base. Cut them out using the craft knife and ruler.

2 Cut out a rectangle of blue paper measuring 3¾ × 7¼ in (9.5 × 18.5cm) and a rectangle of cream card measuring 4 × 7½ in (10 × 19cm). Stick them together using the glue stick.

3 Stick the green triangles to the front of this panel with glue stick, and then glue the base in position.

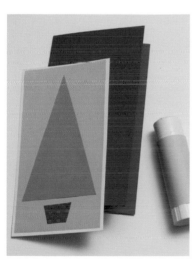

Tip
Use silvers and golds for a more traditional Christmas theme, adding sequins and flat beads to decorate.

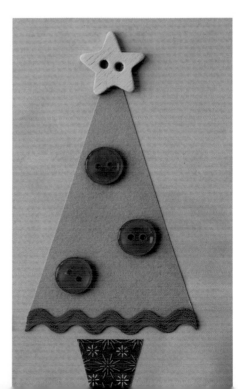

4 Cut out a rectangle of red card measuring 8 × 8½ in (20.5 × 22cm). Score down the center, 4¼ in (11cm) from each side, and fold in half. Apply glue stick to the back of the decorated panel and glue to the front of the red card.

5 Decorate the tree with buttons, rickrack, or bobble braid, gluing in place with craft glue. Finish the card with a star-shaped button on the top of the tree.

Glitter Star Card

Add sparkle to the festivities with these glittery star cards.
Cut a card rectangle, make two folds to form flaps at the front, add a glittery dot to close
the flaps, and the card can be mailed as it is, with the name and address written on the back.
Glitter is available in a wide range of colors—team it with a background paper of a similar hue.

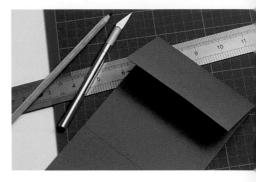

1 Photocopy the template on page 156, cut out the star shape, and draw this onto a piece of paper. Cut out with a craft knife and ruler. Add a few drops of water to a saucer of craft glue to dilute it slightly.

2 Paint a thin coat of glue onto the star, ensuring even coverage. Place on scrap paper, sprinkle over glitter and shake slightly so the glitter covers the entire star. Shake off excess glitter and pour back into the pot. Let the star dry.

3 Cut a piece of colored card measuring 4¾ × 9½in (12 × 24cm). Measure 2½in (6cm) from each side and score gently. Fold the card to make three panels.

4 Measure and cut a square of silver paper 4in (10cm) square using the craft knife and metal ruler. Stick this inside the card, using the glue stick

5 Using undiluted craft glue, stick the star to the center of the square. Draw a ⅝-in (15-mm) diameter circle on scrap paper and paint with diluted craft glue. Sprinkle glitter onto the circle and allow to dry.

6 Stick half of the circle onto one side of one front flap and put a very small dab of glue stick onto the other half. Press down. The card will be held closed but will still open easily without tearing.

Materials

Thin colored card

Glitter in similar colors
to the card

Silver paper

Pencil

White craft glue

Small pot for the glue

Paintbrush

Glue stick

Scrap paper

Craft knife, cutting mat,
and metal ruler

Tip

Instead of using glitter,
simply cut a star shape
from metallic paper and
stick into the card.

Christmas Stocking Card

Give a Christmas stocking with a difference.

These cards will add festive cheer to any mantelpiece. Using a traditional Christmas color scheme of red and white, they make the perfect card for a child but will be equally loved by adults, too. Use store-bought gift-wrap papers or decorate plain red and white card with adhesive stickers. The addition of ribbon and braid finishes the cards off beautifully.

Materials

Thin card in white and red

Red and white patterned gift wrap

Red and white circular stickers

Red crepe paper

Needle and red thread

A selection of braids and ribbons

Craft knife and cutting mat

Glue stick

Fast-drying, high-tack craft glue

Rotary hole punch

Scissors

Tip

Make a large quantity of these stocking cards and send one to each member of the family so they can be suspended in one long line above the fireplace as festive decorations.

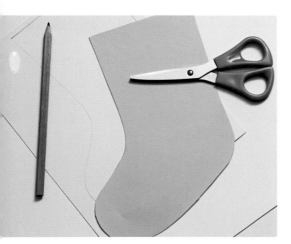

1 Photocopy the stocking template on page 156. Using the template, draw and cut out stocking shapes from the white and red card.

2 For the spotted stockings, stick circular stickers randomly all over one side of the card stocking. Alternatively, draw around the template onto patterned paper and cut out. Glue this onto a plain card stocking with glue stick.

3 Cut a 12 x 1-in (30.5 x 2.5-cm) strip of crepe paper. Stitch along one long edge, securing the thread with a knot at the start. Pleat the paper as you go by gathering it until it measures 4⅜in (11cm). Finish with a few stitches or a knot.

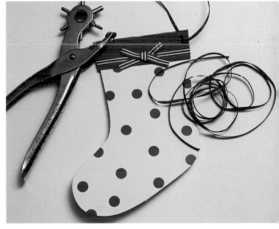

4 Cut out a cuff from either red or white card (the opposite color to the main stocking). Apply craft glue along the bottom of the cuff and glue the crepe paper ruffle along this, if using.

5 Glue the cuff onto the stocking and decorate with lengths of ribbon and braid, adding a ribbon bow if desired.

6 Using the hole punch, make a hole in the top corner of the stocking. Cut a 6in (15.25cm) length of thin red ribbon and thread it through the hole. Tie a neat knot in the ribbon and trim the ends to even them.

Christmas Bauble Card

Use bauble shapes to make these sumptous greetings cards.

Richly patterned papers are teamed with co-ordinating plain card, finished off with a beautiful velvet ribbon trim. Cut out and decorate several bauble shapes, then arrange them onto cards, using two or three together or varying the colors and patterns for some truly unique cards.

Materials

Thin gold card

Patterned gift-wrap,
    preferably metallic

Plain co-ordinating
    paper or thin card

Velvet ribbon

Thin gold ribbon

Craft knife, cutting mat,
    and metal ruler

Scissors

Pencil

Rotary hole punch

Glue stick

Fast-drying, high-tack
    craft glue

Tip

Rather than using ribbon cut to the width of each bauble, cut lengths of ribbon slightly longer than required, glue onto the baubles, and then trim for a neater finsh.

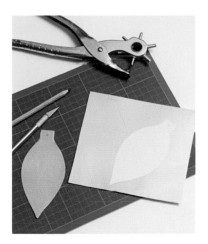

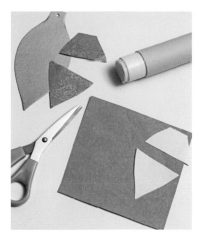

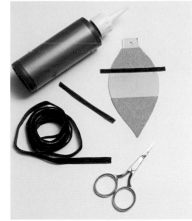

1 Photocopy the template on page 157 and cut out the bauble shape and the shapes for the decorated paper. Draw around the bauble onto gold card and cut out with a craft knife or scissors. Make a small hole with the hole punch at the top of the bauble.

2 Using the templates, cut out paper shapes and glue onto the bauble with glue stick. Press firmly to ensure a good adhesion.

3 Cut 2¾-in (7-cm) lengths of ribbon and glue along the edges of the paper with craft glue. Trim the ends with scissors.

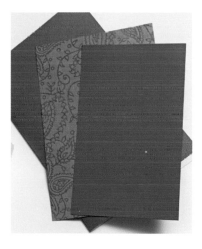

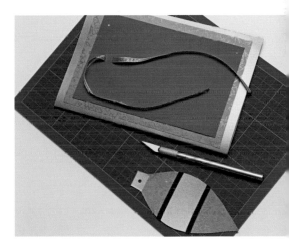

4 Cut out a rectangle of plain paper measuring 4⅜ × 7in (11 × 18cm) and a rectangle of patterned paper measuring 7½ × 5in (19 × 13cm).

5 Cut out a rectangle of gold card measuring 8¼ × 11in (21 × 28cm). Score along the center of the card 5½ in (14cm) in from each long side and fold in half. Glue the patterned rectangle and the plain rectangle centrally onto the front of the card.

6 Cut two slits in the center of the card, wide enough for the ribbon, one 1½ in (4cm) from the top and the other 2in (5cm) from the top. Thread a 10-in (25-cm) length of gold ribbon through the slits from front to back, and through to the front again. Tie the bauble in place with a bow. Trim the ribbon so the ends are even.

Glittery Bird Card

Here a simple bird motif has been enhanced

with glittery papers and ribbons and plumes of silver tissue paper. For a Christmassy look, choose metallic papers, or try a selection of co-ordinating papers in browns and reds for a subtle effect or bright colors for a modern look.

Materials

Thin cream card

Glittery or patterned paper

Gold and silver gift-wrap

Silver crepe paper

Gold star sequins

Silver and gold ribbon, about ⅛in (3mm) wide

Fast-drying, high-tack craft glue

Glue stick

Craft knife, cutting mat, and metal ruler

Scissors (optional)

Pinking shears

Pencil

1 Photocopy the template on page 157, cut out, and lay onto cream card. Carefully draw around the template and cut out neatly with a craft knife or sharp scissors.

2 Cut a beak in metallic paper and a wing in glittery paper. Glue onto the bird. Using pinking shears, cut two strips of metallic paper ½in (1cm) wide and glue across the neck and tail. Stick ribbon on top.

3 Cut two 1¼ x 2¾-in (3 x 7-cm) strips of silver crepe paper. Gather them along one long edge, holding firmly to crease them slightly. Glue one onto the back of the bird at the head and one at the tail. Hold in place until firmly stuck. Glue a sequin onto the bird for the eye.

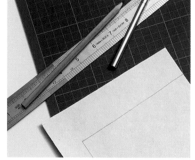

4 Measure and cut out a 4 x 5½-in (10 x 14-cm) rectangle of glittery paper. Measure and cut an 8½ x 6-in (22 x 15.25-cm) rectangle of cream card, score centrally 4¼in (11cm) from each side, and fold in half.

5 Apply the glue stick to the back of the glittery rectangle and stick onto the front of the card. Glue the bird into the center of this and glue ribbon around the edge of the glittery paper, ensuring a straight finish.

Pop-up Gingerbread House Card

Give a housewarming card
with a difference with this cute pop-up gingerbread
house. White rickrack braid and scallop-edged paper are
used to great effect on the roof and around the door, and
as windowframes to resemble the frosting on an edible
gingerbread house, and the card is backed with a soft,
candy-colored paper. Finish off this unique greetings
card with a paper heart stuck to the door to
welcome new visitors.

Materials

Thin brown card

Thin metallic card

Pastel colored glittery paper

Thin rickrack braid

Plain paper

Scallop-bladed scissors

Pencil

Craft knife, cutting mat, and
    metal ruler

Glue stick

Fast-drying, high-tack craft glue

Scissors

Tip

If you wish, for an alternative
look, turn this card into a
traditional country cottage by
decorating the front of the card
with flowers and foliage.

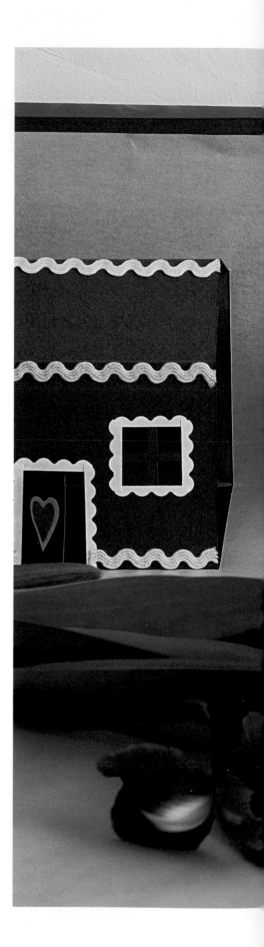

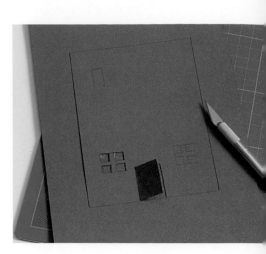

1 Cut out a rectangle of brown card measuring 6¼ × 9½in (16 × 24cm). Draw a pencil line 2in (5cm) in from each short edge. Draw a pencil line 1¼in (3cm) in from each long edge to form a rectangle measuring 4 × 5½in (10 × 14cm) in the middle of the card.

2 Cut down both vertical lines of the inner rectangle with a craft knife and ruler. Measure a line 1⅜in (3.5cm) down from the top of the rectangle and another line 3in (7.5cm) from the top of the rectangle. Score along these and the top and bottom of the rectangle.

3 Draw two windows, a door, and a chimney onto the rectangle and cut out, ensuring that only three sides of the door are cut and one of the vertical sides is kept intact.

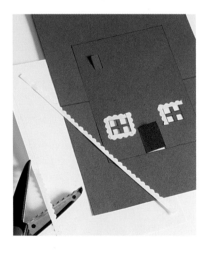

4 Measure and score a line centrally on each side of the house 4¾in (12cm) from the top and bottom.

5 Cut strips of white paper ¼in (7mm) wide and then cut along one side with scalloped scissors. Cut into short lengths and, using the glue stick, attach them around the windows and door and to the top of the chimney.

6 Using craft glue, stick rickrack along the roof, the top of the house, and the bottom of the house each side of the door. You will need about 12in (30.5cm) of rickrack, so the ends can be trimmed neatly.

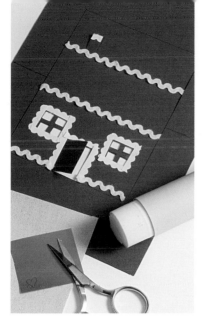

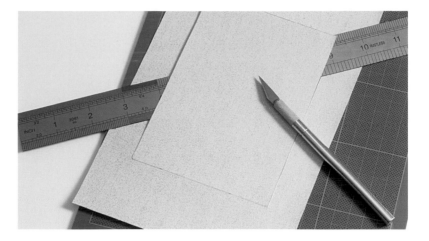

7 Cut out a small heart from the metallic paper and a slightly smaller one from glittery paper. Using the glue stick, stick them to the door.

8 Cut a rectangle of glittery paper measuring 6 x 9in (15.25 x 23cm). Measure and draw a line 1¾in (4.5cm) in from the top and the bottom of the rectangle and a line on each side 1in (2.5cm) in from the edge. Cut out this rectangle using a craft knife, metal ruler, and cutting mat. Apply glue stick to the back of this and glue onto the brown card over the house.

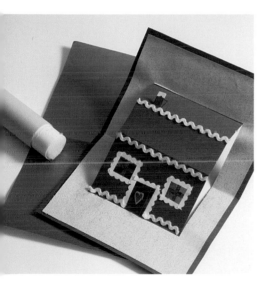

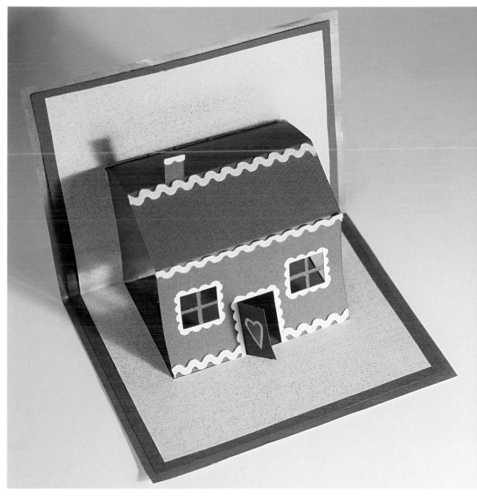

9 Cut a rectangle of metallic card measuring 6½ x 10in (16.5 x 25.5cm). Score a line horizontally 5in (12.5cm) from the top and bottom. Apply glue stick to the back of the brown card and stick onto the metallic card, ensuring an even border all the way around. Bend the card along all the score lines so that the house stands out from the card.

Tasseled Key Card

Give someone the key to the door with this unusual card, ideal for a new-house greeting. Muted colors have been used here for an understated, classic appearance, and a large cardboard key, topped off with a tassel made from thin satin ribbon, is used as a key fob. Use the templates provided at the back of the book or look out for old keys to base your design on, bearing in mind that the more intricate the pattern, the trickier it will be to cut out.

Materials

Thin card in purple, blue, cream, gray, and gold
Rotary hole punch
⅛-in (3-mm) wide ribbon
Scrap card
Scissors
Pinking shears
Craft knife, cutting mat, and metal ruler
Glue stick

Tip

This design would also work very well as a "coming of age" card, to celebrate an eighteenth or twenty-first birthday.

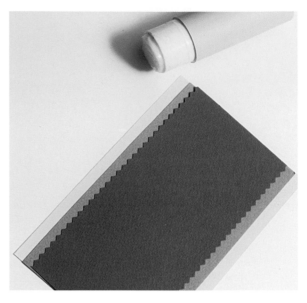

1 Cut out a rectangle of purple card measuring 3¼ x 6¼in (8 x 16cm). Draw a line ¼in (7mm) in from each long edge. Cut along this line with pinking shears to make a jagged edge.

2 Cut out a rectangle of blue card measuring 3½ x 6¼in (9 x 16cm). Cut out a rectangle of cream card measuring 4¼ x 6¼in (10.5 x 16cm). Glue the purple strip onto the blue strip with glue stick and then glue this onto the cream strip, ensuring that the borders at the top and bottom are equal.

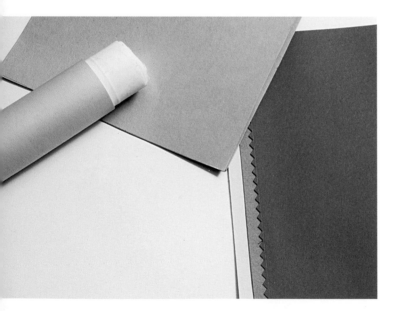

3 Cut out a rectangle of gray card measuring 5½ x 12½in (14 x 32cm). Score down the center of the card lengthways, 6¼in (16cm) from either edge and fold in half. Glue the colored strips onto the front of this using the glue stick.

4 Photocopy the template of a key on page 158, cut it out, and draw around it onto gold card. Using a craft knife, slowly and carefully cut it out. Punch a small hole at the top with the hole punch.

5 To make a tassel, cut a piece of scrap card 2¾ × 4in (7 × 10cm) and fold in half lengthways. Cut a 4¾-in (12-cm) length of ribbon and another piece 30in (76cm) long. Tape each end of the short ribbon to the folded edge of the card. Holding the end of the long ribbon at the bottom of the card, wrap the ribbon around the card.

6 Remove the tape from the short piece of ribbon and tie the ribbon firmly at the top with a double knot, leaving the ends long. Push a blade of the scissors between the two pieces of card at the opposite end to the tied ribbon and cut through the ribbon. Remove the card.

7 Tie a short length of ribbon around the tassel and secure with a neat knot. Tie the ribbon at the top of the tassel through the hole in the key and trim the ends neatly. Glue the key and tassel onto the card with glue stick.

Ribbon Notelet

Send a quick note of thanks on these tasteful notelets.

Choose smart gift-wrap papers and finish off with a length of beautiful ribbon. These notelets are just perfect for showing your gratitude to friends and loved ones.

Materials

Thin cream card
Two patterned gift-
    wraps
Cream paper
14in (36cm) of ribbon,
    1in (2.5cm) wide
Rotary hole punch
Craft knife, cutting mat,
    and metal ruler
Glue stick

Tip

Instead of using as a notelet with plain paper, attach a favorite photograph or picture instead.

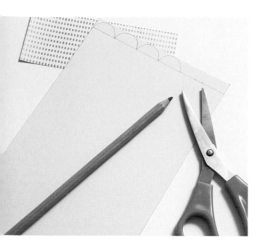

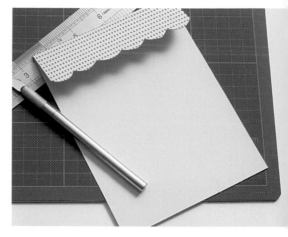

1 Cut out a rectangle of card measuring 4¾ × 8in (12 × 20.5cm). Draw a line ½in (1cm) in from one end, divide the width of the card into six, and draw a scalloped shape in each section. Cut out a rectangle of patterned paper measuring 4¾ × 2in (12 × 5cm) and glue onto the end of the cream card, on the other side to the drawn scallops.

2 Cut out the scalloped edge with a craft knife or scissors.

3 Score a line 1½in (4cm) from the bottom of the scalloped edge, and fold along the line with the patterned side uppermost.

4 Cut out a rectangle of patterned paper measuring 4¾ × 6¼in (12 × 16cm) and stick onto the cream card under the flap, using glue stick.

5 Cut out a piece of cream paper measuring 3½ × 5½in (9 × 14cm). Place this centrally under the flap. Punch two holes 1in (2.5cm) apart and ¾in (2cm) from the top fold.

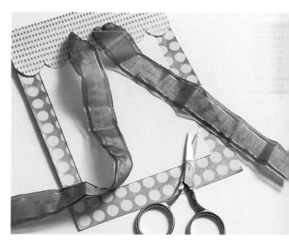

6 Thread ribbon through the holes and tie with a bow. Trim the ribbon ends to make them the same length.

Templates

The templates featured on
the following pages can either be photocopied or traced for use
in the projects. All are featured at the correct size, apart from the
Handbag Card and the Peg Doll Card—these are shown at half
the original size, but they can easily be photocopied at 200% to
increase them to the size required by the project. You can also
use the shapes and outlines on these pages to create greetings
cards of your own design.

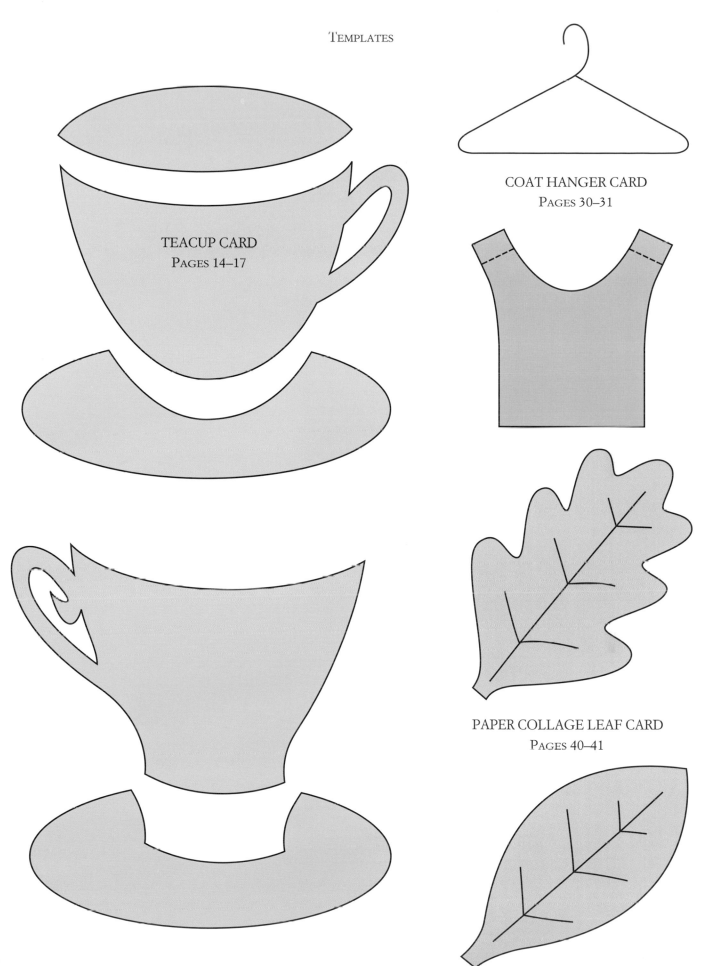

TEACUP CARD
PAGES 14–17

COAT HANGER CARD
PAGES 30–31

PAPER COLLAGE LEAF CARD
PAGES 40–41

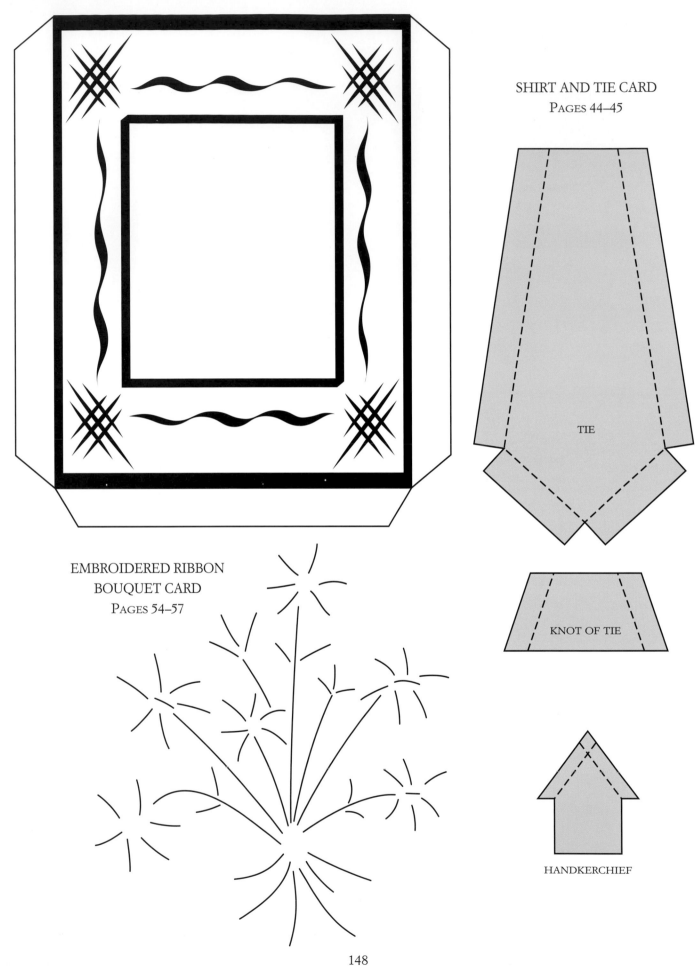

SHIRT AND TIE CARD
PAGES 44–45

TIE

KNOT OF TIE

HANDKERCHIEF

EMBROIDERED RIBBON
BOUQUET CARD
PAGES 54–57

148

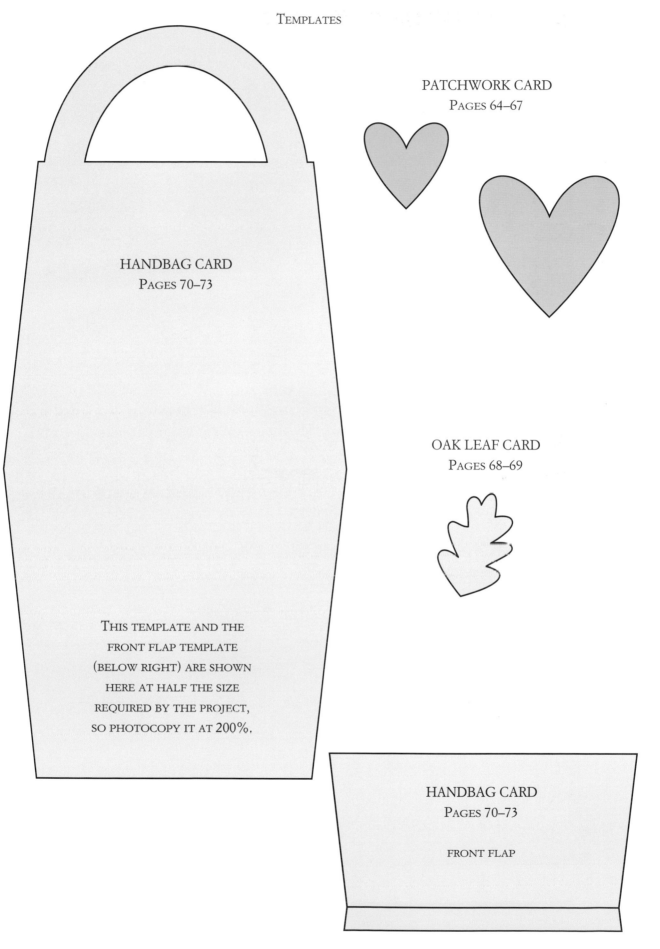

PATCHWORK CARD
PAGES 64–67

HANDBAG CARD
PAGES 70–73

OAK LEAF CARD
PAGES 68–69

THIS TEMPLATE AND THE
FRONT FLAP TEMPLATE
(BELOW RIGHT) ARE SHOWN
HERE AT HALF THE SIZE
REQUIRED BY THE PROJECT,
SO PHOTOCOPY IT AT 200%.

HANDBAG CARD
PAGES 70–73

FRONT FLAP

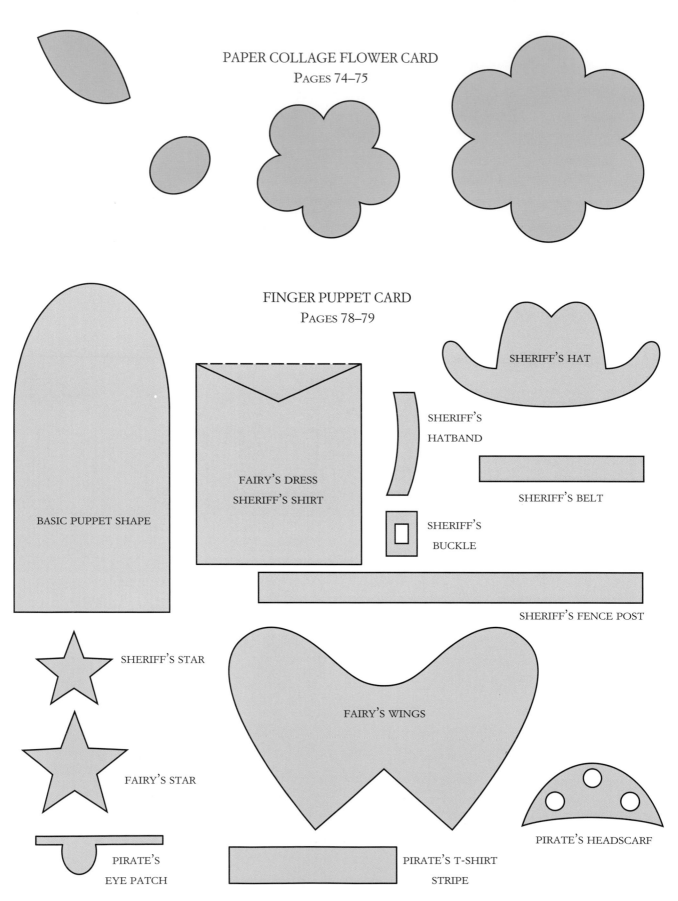

PAPER COLLAGE FLOWER CARD
PAGES 74–75

FINGER PUPPET CARD
PAGES 78–79

SHERIFF'S HAT

SHERIFF'S HATBAND

SHERIFF'S BELT

FAIRY'S DRESS
SHERIFF'S SHIRT

SHERIFF'S BUCKLE

BASIC PUPPET SHAPE

SHERIFF'S FENCE POST

SHERIFF'S STAR

FAIRY'S STAR

FAIRY'S WINGS

PIRATE'S HEADSCARF

PIRATE'S EYE PATCH

PIRATE'S T-SHIRT STRIPE

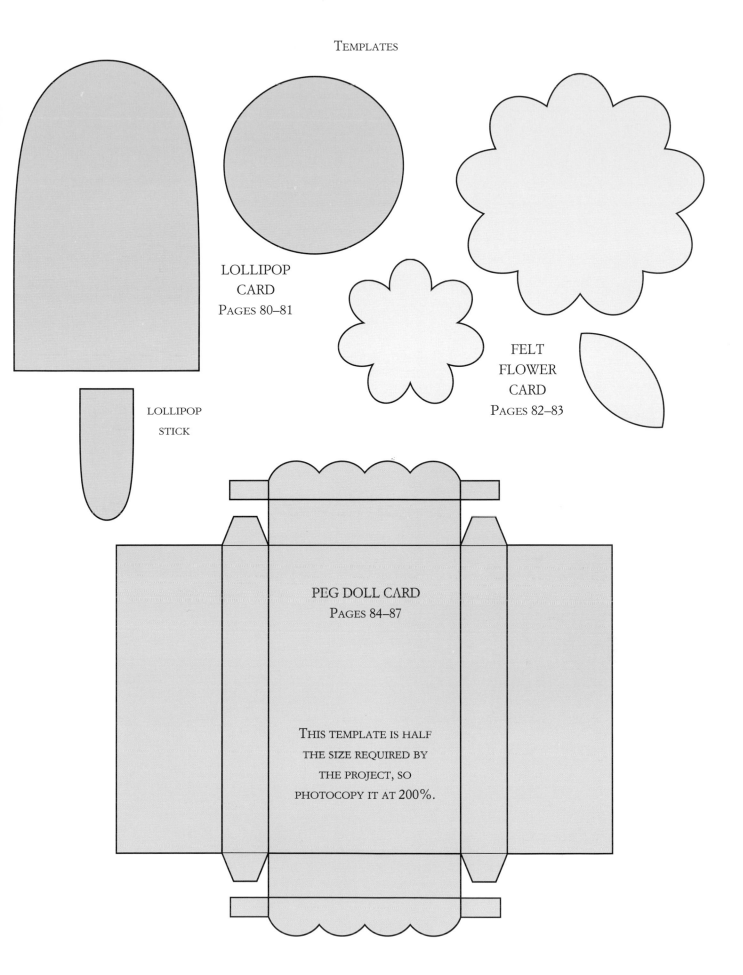

LOLLIPOP
CARD
PAGES 80–81

LOLLIPOP
STICK

FELT
FLOWER
CARD
PAGES 82–83

PEG DOLL CARD
PAGES 84–87

THIS TEMPLATE IS HALF
THE SIZE REQUIRED BY
THE PROJECT, SO
PHOTOCOPY IT AT 200%.

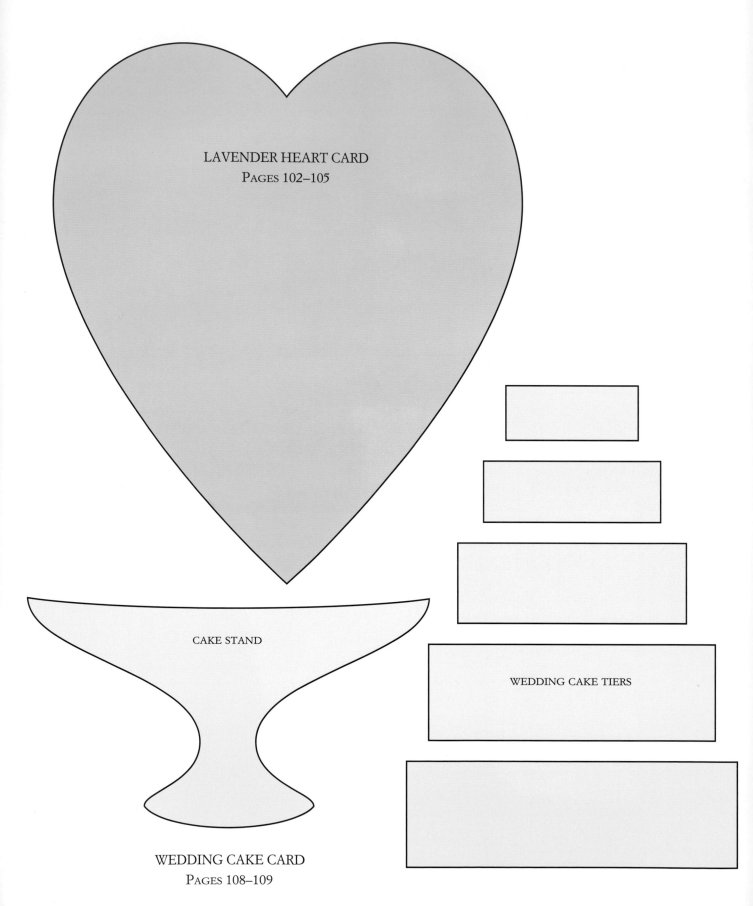

LAVENDER HEART CARD
PAGES 102–105

CAKE STAND

WEDDING CAKE TIERS

WEDDING CAKE CARD
PAGES 108–109

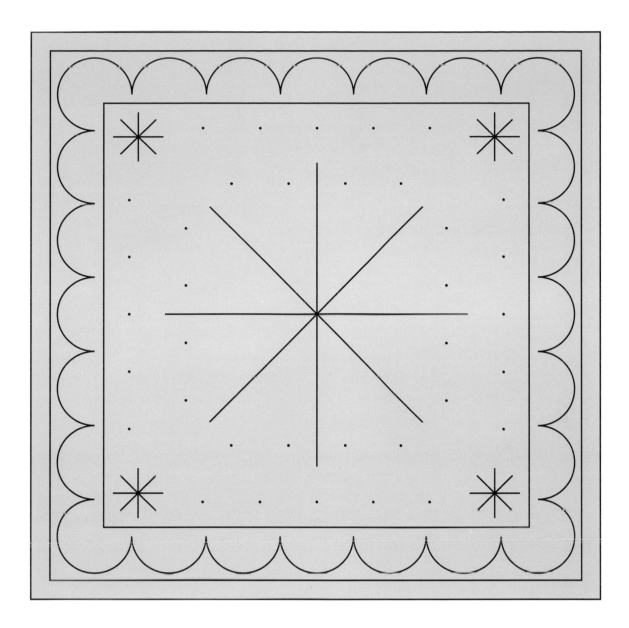

PIN-HOLE CARD
PAGES 106–107

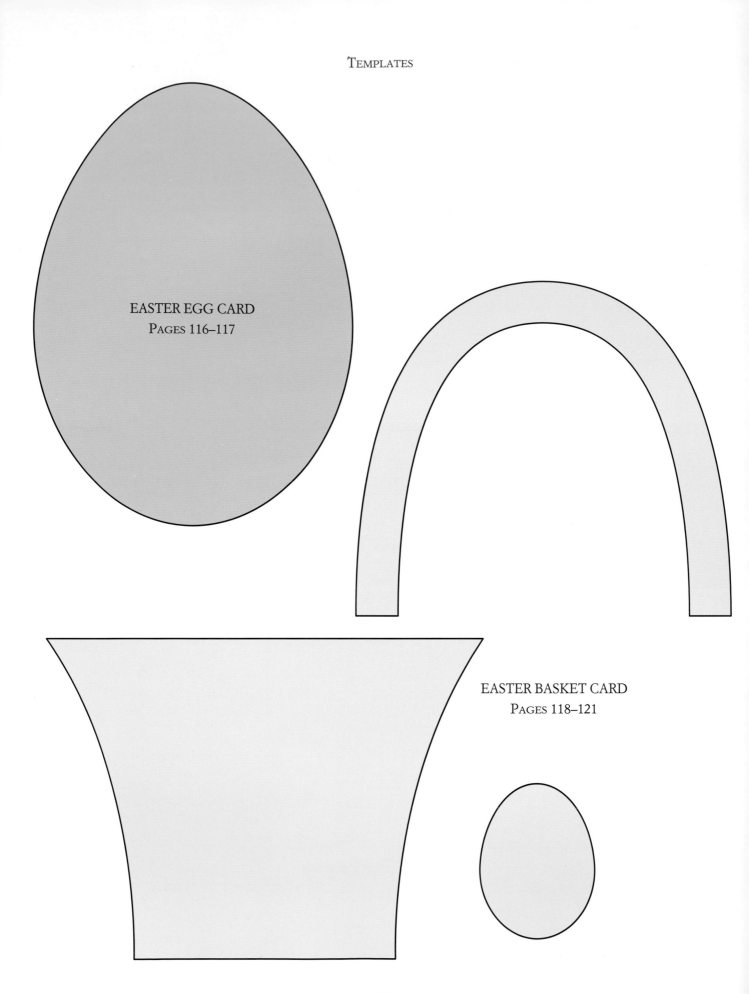

EASTER EGG CARD
PAGES 116–117

EASTER BASKET CARD
PAGES 118–121

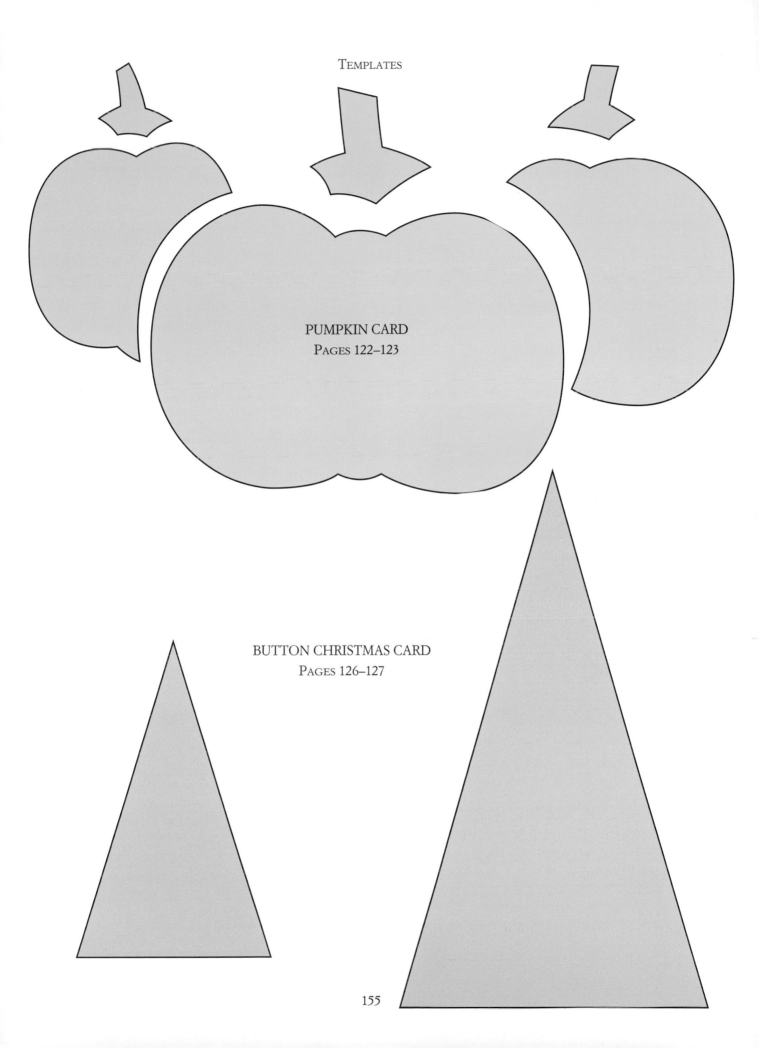

PUMPKIN CARD
PAGES 122–123

BUTTON CHRISTMAS CARD
PAGES 126–127

155

GLITTER STAR CARD
PAGES 128–129

CHRISTMAS STOCKING CARD
PAGES 130–131

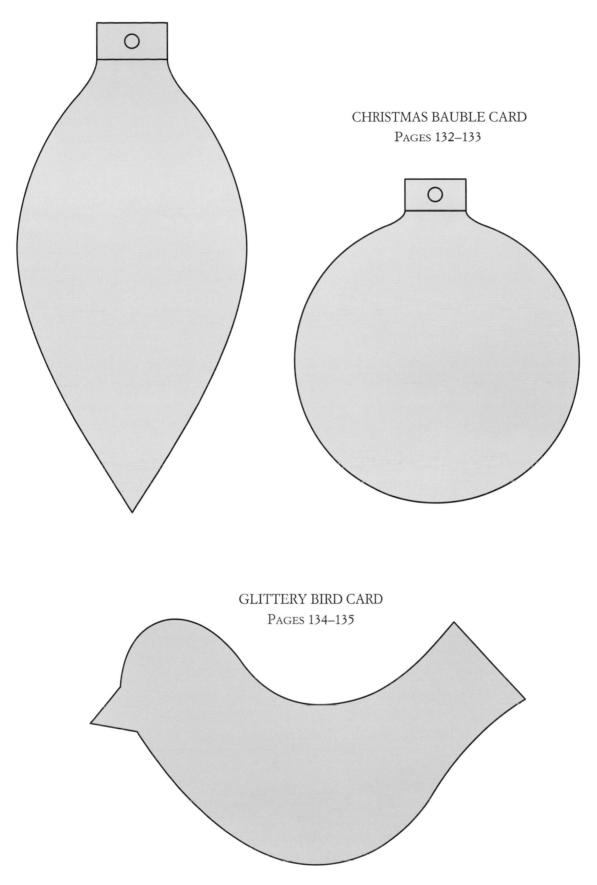

CHRISTMAS BAUBLE CARD
PAGES 132–133

GLITTERY BIRD CARD
PAGES 134–135

TASSELED KEY CARD
Pages 140–143

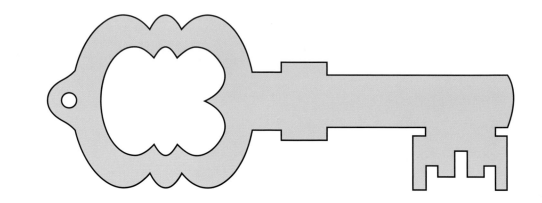

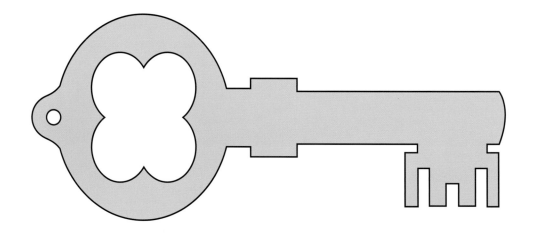

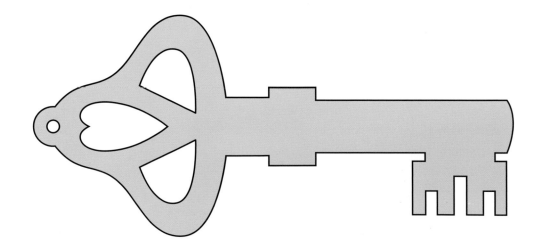

Index

Author's Acknowledgments

Thank you to Gloria Nicol for the lovely Vintage Fabric Card, Vintage Wallpaper Card, Frame Card, and Vintage Flower Button Card. Many thanks to Tino Tedaldi for beautiful photography and for such good humor during the step-by-step photography, and to Gillian Haslam for being a great editor and for helping to juggle photography and baby care with such understanding and patience. Thank you to Cindy Richards and Georgina Harris at Cico Books for their help, enthusiasm, and encouragement, and for commissioning me to do this book in the first place. Thanks, also, to Jacqui Hurst for additional photography. And finally, a very big thank you and all my love to Laurie, Gracie, and Betty for all their help, love, and support.